# Make Up Your Mind!

# Make Up Your Mind!

## The Seven Building Blocks to Better Decisions

John D. Arnold

**amacom**

A Division of American Management Associations

**Library of Congress Cataloging in Publication Data**

Arnold, John D
  Make up your mind!

  Includes index.
  1. Decision-making.      I. Title.
HD30.23.A73            640            78–16253
ISBN 0–8144–5479–8

Second Printing

*To*
*Dotti, Derek, Keith, and Craig*

# Preface

"It's only with the heart we can see. What is essential is invisible to the eye."
— Antoine de Saint-Exupéry, *The Little Prince*

The late French writer Saint-Exupery was not even remotely thinking of the subject of this book when he penned those words more than 30 years ago. But the sentiments he expressed explain what is wrong with most books about decision making: they are based on the questionable assumption that the most logical or rational decision is also the most effective.

That assumption ignores the fact that the success of a decision often depends on factors other than pure logic or reason—on our emotions, beliefs, values, and attitudes and those of the people on whose cooperation our decision depends.

*Make Up Your Mind* is written in the belief that the most effective decisions integrate thinking and feelings and take into account the thinking and feelings of others. The book presents a system for decision making that enables you to strike a balance between your logic and your emotions. It gives you a personal process—an individualized instrument—for making decisions that reflect your style and your values. It recognizes the fact that you are the world's leading authority on yourself and that you are already familiar with most of the elements of effective decision making. What you need is a way to organize what you know, to structure your thinking.

The Seven ExecuTrak Building Blocks provide such a structure. A major element of the ExecuTrak Systems™ for Managing Change, which have been used successfully by leaders of many of the world's largest multinational corporations, they provide a powerful tool that can help you decide what you want—from your job, your marriage, even your life.

The book flows from two separate streams in my own background. The first is personal, the second professional.

To take the personal first: I started work in a factory when I was 12, sorting leather into separate grades. I worked through shipping and production into sales and marketing. Later, in college, I set up and managed a magazine subscription agency covering Boston-area colleges, sold shoes and infants' wear, and led a seven-piece jazz band. I spent two summers of my four years at Harvard hitchhiking the nation. I traveled 13,500 miles and met my expenses by harvesting lettuce and cherries and working as a short-order chef and gardener. In my travels I met hundreds of people from all walks of life: land developers and longshoremen, ranchers and fieldhands, debutantes and drifters.

All these experiences convinced me of one fact: most people use only a small part of their talent and potential in everyday life.

Many people lead lives, if not of quiet desperation—as Henry David Thoreau said—then at least of persistent compromise. They compromise their true potential because of what they have come to accept as their "true lot in life."

Before I finished college, I resolved to try to make a significant contribution to helping men and women capitalize on their full talents to achieve more satisfying lives. But how? The answer lies in the second stream from which this book flows: my profession.

My firm, John Arnold ExecuTrak Systems, provides confidential management counseling services to business and government executives, people whose base salaries range to $750,000 a year and more. We help them manage major changes in their organizations in response to changes in the marketplace, government regulations, consumer lifestyles, and technological or competitive breakthroughs.

What we do for our clients sounds simple: we help them "think things through," structuring their analysis of the issues and opportunities they face to clarify their objectives and devise innovative ways of achieving those objectives. To put it another way, we work as sounding board, diagnostician, troubleshooter, and catalyst to help them and their management teams find solutions that best meet their needs.

A worldwide paper company needed to turn around a deteriorating earnings picture in one of its divisions. We helped identify new opportunities and ways to exploit them that enabled the division to meet its profit plan just four months later and achieve a 16 percent return on investment at the end of the year. We helped a multinational packaging corporation integrate a European subsidiary, a food company save $22 million by thinking through a key capital investment decision, a grain processor streamline its organization, and a steel company devise and implement a strategy that won it an $88 million contract. (For a fuller description of ExecuTrak methods, see Appendix C.)

Gradually, executives who had asked us to help solve their business problems began asking us to help solve their personal problems as well. As a personal favor to clients, I have guided their children in choosing a college, their wives in going back to work, and themselves in coping with a career move. Many of these clients have since adopted the Seven ExecuTrak Building Blocks in their own lives, having discovered that they are as applicable to making everyday personal decisions as they are to making multimillion-dollar business decisions.

With this book, the same techniques they have used effectively can be yours. By learning the Seven Building Blocks—and equally important, learning how to apply them—you can better manage your own life and make a more meaningful contribution to the lives of those you work with and those you love.

The book is divided into five sections. Section I (Chapters 1-3) explains why you need a systematic method for making decisions and sets forth the basic concepts on which ExecuTrak is based. Section II (Chapters 4-11) presents the Seven ExecuTrak Building Blocks and teaches you how to apply them to any situation you may want to resolve.

Section III (Chapters 12-14) describes how the Building Blocks can help you resolve a variety of situations you face every day, from drawing up a family budget to buying a washing machine, from making the most of your leisure time to spending your bonus. It also demonstrates how you can use the Building Blocks under stress, when there is "no time to think."

Section IV (Chapters 15-16) shows how men and women have applied these decision-making techniques to highly personal and emotional issues. A teenager used them to think through what to do about her baby. A man used them to help determine how to save a broken marriage. Section V (Chapters 17-20) demonstrates how you can use the Building Blocks to clarify your career ambitions and find the right job.

In the Appendixes you will find a glossary of terms used throughout this book and handy checklists to guide you in buying a car, buying a house, choosing a college, and drawing up a family budget. You will also find a concise listing of the many applications of ExecuTrak methodology as used by many people in their work.

This book provides a systematic way of looking at problems and opportunities that will enable you to make better decisions. Once you understand the system, improving your decision-making skills is only a matter of practice. This process can be accelerated and reinforced by participating in a self-study program or seminar on decision making.

I am indebted to the following people for their important role in shaping this book. Peter Arnold and George Gross, who helped in the early stages of its development; Marlies Wolfenden and especially Anne Mooradian, whose typing and incisive questions helped to sharpen its focus; and Mark Arnold, whose influence helped make it a better book.

If you are concerned with gaining greater mastery over your life, this book is written for you. Today is the first day of the rest of your life—what an opportunity!

JOHN D. ARNOLD

# Contents

**Section V**
Clarifying Your Career Ambitions; Planning Your Life Goals

# Section I

## Why You Need a Systematic Approach to Decision Making

# 1

## What You Choose
## Is What You Are

"Darling," a friend of mine asked her husband, "do you have trouble making decisions?"

He thought a moment. "Well, yes and no."

"Well, at least you didn't say you wanted to sleep on it," she responded.

Making decisions is something we all have to do hundreds of times a week. Most decisions have little lasting effect. Should you mop the kitchen floor or watch TV? Have dinner at home or eat out? Other decisions can change your life. Should you ask for a raise or quit your job? Rent a cottage at the lake or build a small summer home? Invest in municipal bonds for current income or in a real estate tax shelter for future income? Marry the man or woman you love or postpone marriage to finish school or start a career? Such decisions can deeply affect your future happiness.

Considering all the practice we get in making decisions, you would expect that we would be good at making them: the more typing you do, the better typist you become. But the number of decisions you make has *nothing* to do with your skill at making them or the results you obtain. For the most part, decision making is an ignored art. We take lessons to learn tennis or golf, but we rely on our own devices to learn how to make decisions. It is assumed that decision making comes naturally, like learning to breathe. It does not.

3

Most of the books on decision making are addressed to businesspeople, as though they were the only ones who had important decisions to make. Yet the decisions you make about your life are as important to you as a multimillion-dollar decision is to someone in business. How you make them can determine whether or not you achieve a satisfying life.

Most of the "authorities" on successful living tell us that their particular specialty—religion, philosophy, sex, education, gamesmanship, or the latest psychological fad—holds the key to a successful life. But after you have taken their courses and read their books, you are left with the burden of having to make decisions about religion, philosophy, sex, education, gamesmanship, or the latest psychological fad. *A system for making decisions can be the key to all the other keys.*

Frequently, we are not even consciously aware that big decisions have to be made, or that we have the power to make them. I remember the first job I had, when I was 12, sorting hides in a shoe factory. I had to decide which were soft enough, thin enough, and smooth enough for uppers. The hides would arrive in heavy, smelly bundles, tied with rope. I cut the binding, let the bundle fly open, and began making little decisions.

If a hide was stiff, thick, and slightly blemished, I tossed it in the pile for soles. When the cutter picked it up, he decided the best way to cut it to get the most soles and the least waste. The cutting machines pounded, the workers yelled to one another above the noise, the smell of tanning dyes filled the air, and the flies buzzed. The cutter and I continued to make decisions. The rule was to get the most usable leather from each hide. The outcome, if we made good decisions, was that the company would make a profit and we would get to keep our jobs.

But we had bigger decisions to make where the rules and outcome were not so obvious. At 35 cents an hour, was my job the best way to accumulate $18.75 for the government savings bond I had as my objective? Even if I drank water on my Coke break instead of Coke? And what of the cutter? Should he spend the rest of his life in a monotonous job, sucking on an unlit cigar to help numb his sense of smell? Should the stitcher let her eyesight deteriorate under the strain of close work and inferior lighting? No one openly addressed these questions. If any decisions were made about them, they seemed to be made by default.

At any point in our lives we are the product of all the decisions we have made to date, or the product of our decisions and those decisions we allowed others to make for us. Some of those decisions were right, some wrong, some postponed, and some defaulted. Decisions made by doing nothing, especially career and lifestyle decisions, can have as much impact as ones made by positive action. Yet the sad fact is that most of us tend to drift. We accept conditions the way they are, and the longer we accept them the more difficult it becomes to change them. Like the cutter and the stitcher, we may shrink from addressing the important questions and making the important decisions.

In the course of my life I have heard hundreds of people rationalize their drifting. Their explanations are varied, but they usually come down to this:

"I've never really been able to make up my mind what I want to do."

"I really don't have much choice; I don't have the education;" or "I need the money and I put up with the drudgery because it's a living;" or "I'm discriminated against because of my age, color, or sex."

"I know what I want to do, but I don't see any way to do it."

If you find echoes of your own thinking in those statements, you are reading the right book. You will see that indeed you do have choices, that you can control your own life. You will learn the process of decision making used by many senior executives in business and government, and by men and women in their everyday lives.

If a man places a gun to your forehead and threatens to pull the trigger unless you tell him what he wants to know, your first reaction may be that you have no choice. Yet if you systematically put your mind to it, you will see that you have at least seven choices. Which one you select depends on your character, values, and circumstances:

1. Patrick Henry would probably have said, "Shoot," thus putting the decision up to the gunman.
2. Benedict Arnold would probably have said, "What you want to know is right here in my coat pocket," and handed it over.
3. John Paul Jones would probably have disarmed the gunman and held him as a hostage.
4. Baron Munchausen, the famous teller of tall tales, would probably have said, "Of course I will tell you," and then lied.
5. Ben Franklin would probably have said, "Can't we talk this over?"
6. Mortimer Snerd, the lovable scatterbrained dummy, would probably have said, "I seem to disremember. What was the question?"
7. Rip Van Winkle would probably have said, "I'll give you my answer tomorrow. I want to sleep on it."

With a gun pressed against your head, your seven choices are (1) defiance, (2) surrender, (3) counterattack, (4) lying, (5) reasoning, (6) pleading ignorance, and (7) stalling. On different occasions in your life, have you not resorted to them all?

A dramatization of a similar situation was responsible for one of the biggest laughs in radio history. Pointing a gun at his victim, a robber threatened, "Your money or your life." In his role as the world's stingiest man, Jack Benny silently debated with himself. Even though there was no punchline, the pause was filled with audience laughter. When the threat to his life was repeated, Benny responded, "Don't rush me. I'm thinking it over."

He knew he had a decision to make, and so do you have decisions to make, even when you think there may be none. If the possibilities when you are confronted with a gun are seven, how many more are there in any problem you may be wrestling with now—if only you knew how to look for them?

That you do not recognize your choices or that you have no organized method of making decisions is not surprising. Decision making is not taught in schools. Many of the books on the subject, usually texts for business courses, seem to preach platitudes. Often they deal with theory, not practice. They tell us to define the problem, get the facts, analyze the facts, weigh the advantages and disadvantages, and then make a decision. Such advice is about as helpful as a book on swimming is to a drowning man.

What is the result of this vacuum of instruction on decision making? Many of us do not know how to make up our minds. Should we buy a car, quit our job, try to understand what's bothering our mate? Some of us never come to any decision at all until the old car breaks down, our employer cuts the payroll, or the divorce proceedings begin.

Some of us tend to make snap decisions without appreciating the consequences. Getting the decision behind us becomes more important than making sure that the decision is a good one. We might just as well flip a coin. In fact, coin flipping is one of the commonest methods of decision making.

Some of us do the opposite. We worry ourselves sick over a decision but put off coming to any conclusion. Like a baby with a bottle, we take up a decision, push it aside after a few minutes, then pick it up again for further fretting. Or we ask the advice of a friend. Unable and untrained to make a decision by ourselves, we seek to share our responsibility with others. Are we really seeking candid advice? Or are we looking for confirmation to reinforce our decision? Are we looking for a scapegoat so that when things go wrong we can say, "Well, Stanley, this is another nice mess you've gotten me into"?

No wonder the advice columns in the newspapers are so well read. They offer a way to get out from under the burden of making our own decisions.

Yet what can a stranger know of our particular situation? Why don't we consult *ourselves*, the world's greatest living authority on the subject? In most cases we do not know how to ask the questions or even what questions to ask. Our overgrown educational establishment, which has difficulty even in teaching Johnny to read, has failed us. It has not taught us how to make up our minds.

Admitting that you are not expert in making decisions need not be fatal to your ego. You are in excellent company. Some of the most successful people in government and industry regularly seek counsel when they face new situations and challenges. Recently I had a call from a man who had just been handpicked by the founder of a giant electronics corporation to take over as president at an annual salary of a quarter of a million dollars. While still in his thirties, he had built a reputation as a Wall Street wizard and the dynamic executive vice president of a multinational conglomerate. Smooth, suave, and self-assured, he is now the kind of man whose career is profiled in such publications as *Business Week* and *Fortune*.

What could he possibly have to worry about? Simply this: in receiving his new appointment, he had been parachuted in over the heads of senior and more experienced executives who felt they had first claim on the presidency when the founder relinquished that job but retained his second hat—board chairman. The founder, a giant in the industry, had a reputation for assigning responsibility but withholding authority. With no background in the industry, the new president was in a precarious position. Two of his subordinates, openly hostile, had told him he would be dead within a month.

What did he want from me? "I've got to figure out," he said, "how to handle a palace revolt by men who think they should have my job. I've got to reassure the chairman that letting go of his authority is the right move, and I've got to demonstrate to the board that my lack of background in electronics will be no handicap. The next 90 days will decide whether I can hack it or not."

As the new president, he could handle his hostile subordinates in several ways. He could conciliate them. He could dominate them. He could even separate them, but he knew they had helped lead the company to the top of the industry. He needed their talent, experience, and commitment. One of the worst things that could happen would be for them to resign and join the competition. He could demand or he could retreat. Which was it to be and why? Would a combination be best? Where should he begin? How should he begin?

The Chinese have a saying that if you give a starving man a fish you keep him from starving for one day, but if you teach him how to fish you keep him from starving for life. As consultant to this extremely able and sucessful executive, I was not going to throw him a fish. Indeed, I had no fish to throw. What I was going to do was to help him learn and apply the principles of good decision making, a skill that would last him all his life. I would serve as his sounding board during an awkward, but critical transition.

We determined that an early task was to find ways of demonstrating to the palace revolutionaries the soundness of his appointment. Somehow, they had to be made to understand why he had been chosen over them. It was natural that they should feel envious of him. He decided that whatever he did, he would do it tactfully and politely, but also with firmness.

He quickly discovered that the revolutionaries, each a prince in his own fiefdom, had little knowledge of the kingdom. Each knew his own little piece of the corporate territory, but not the design that encompassed the whole. Further, while they were used to the trappings of power—the plush offices, the large expense accounts, the private planes—they had not exercised any real power because the founder had held them on short leashes.

Wagon-wheel meetings had been the rule. At a wagon-wheel meeting the boss sits at the hub, with each subordinate at the rim on the end of a spoke. The hub issues instructions to one of the spokes. The spoke says it's a good idea and he will get right on it. He then sits and watches while the hub repeats the procedure with each spoke in the circle. All opportunity for input, all opportunity for interaction, reaction, and synergy is lost.

Under the new president the revolutionaries were introduced to a new kind of meeting where all the participants are able to contribute and to react to the ideas of others. The value lies in interaction. As they exchange ideas, they produce a decision that is greater than the sum of the individual contributions.

At one of the first of these meetings the new president announced: "Some of you may not be happy I'm here, but I'm here, so get used to it. I'm here because I have the confidence of the board chairman. And that means that you and I together can get things done, if we work in partnership. What do I mean by partnership? Simply this: if any program you recommend stands the test of our probing at meetings like this and wins my approval, I'll take responsibility for bringing back the sanction of the board chairman. I hold this management committee accountable only for recommending approval of programs that serve the best interests of the whole corporation. Once

I've agreed to them, you can hold me accountable for convincing the chairman to go ahead with them. If, after I've been here for a while, we find that you're able to convince me but I can't convince him, then I'm not the man for this job, and I'll resign. But as long as I'm here, let's work together."

The idea of anyone guaranteeing to deliver the board chairman's approval was mind-boggling to the princes of the fiefdoms. The idea of anyone offering to resign as king was a demonstration of stature not previously seen in these corporate hills.

The new president introduced the princes to a Group President's Project, a wide-ranging exercise designed to reevaluate the corporate purpose in the light of economic conditions, new trends in the industry, and increasing government regulation. The project required answering such basic questions as "What is our raison d'être?" "What is our business today and what should it be in the future?" "What kind of strategy do we need to become the kind of company we want to be?" "What's the best organizational structure to support this strategy?" The project also sought to identify the strengths and weaknesses of the company and to establish priorities for action.

"This is *our* project," said the new president, "not mine. Your experience, talent, and commitment are vital to its success."

The project, of course, brought the princes out of their fiefdoms and gave them a glimpse of the kingdom. It also made them part of a team effort, spearheaded by the new president to set new directions.

What were the results of the president's efforts? His business strategy led his corporation to record-breaking earnings in a year when his competitors were using a business recession as an excuse for their poor showings. As of this writing, he has produced 18 consecutive quarters of improved earnings. Those who coveted his job now drop his name in conversations to impress their friends. How did he do it? By using the decision-making system explored in this book to identify and resolve the issues and to uncover and exploit hidden opportunities.

This book will give a proven set of decision-making methods that can be applied to any decision you want to make, from "What kind of car should I buy?" to "What do I want to do with my life?" Your new-found decision-making skills can help improve your self-confidence, increase your earning power, and enhance your influence over events and your persuasive power over other people. The system cannot, of course, guarantee your future happiness and success. What it can do is give you the tools to make better decisions. With them, you can gain greater control of your own life.

What you choose is what you are. So get ready. You are about to learn how to *Make Up Your Mind!*

# 2

# Feeling and Thinking

"Give me liberty or give me death" is a value judgment. It says the speaker values liberty more than life. It can lead to a decision for war.

"Better red than dead" is also a value judgment. It says the speaker values life more than liberty. It can lead to a decison to avoid war.

Both of these emotion-laden judgments are extreme and lead to extreme decisions. One decision maker willingly risks death. The other willingly risks authoritarian control. Who has made the correct or appropriate decision? Both decisions are appropriate for the persons who made them, given the circumstances under which they were made, for decision making is an evaluative process. The decisions you make reveal your values. Your values shape your decisions.

The purchase of a Lincoln Continental when the family savings are depleted tells us that the subject values a status symbol more than money in the bank. A trip to the refrigerator by a would-be dieter tells us the subject values a snack more than a narrow waistline.

To make an effective decision, you have to know your values. If a decision or series of decisions is to help you get what you want out of life, you have to decide what it is you want out of life. That is your basic decision. It is, of course, a difficult one, probably the most difficult one in the world. Philosophers, theologians, and mystics have wrestled with it since the beginning of time. "Eat, drink, and be merry, for tomorrow we die" is one answer. "What profits it a man to gain the whole world if he loses his immortal soul?" is another. A thousand other answers lie in between.

If I were to ask you at this particular moment exactly what you want out of life, you could answer either objectively or subjectively, consciously or subconsciously, with your head or with your heart. Which shall it be? Now you have a second decision to make before you can make the first.

Some psychologists maintain that there are two kinds of people, those who are directed mainly by their minds and those who are directed mainly by their emotions. Yet clinical experiments suggest that the human brain has the capacity to operate equally well in both modes. According to one theory, the brain is divided into two distinct hemispheres. One hemisphere controls the logical, conscious, linear functions; the other controls the emotional, subconscious, intuitive functions.

This theory holds that there is a constant struggle between both hemispheres for dominance. When we fly into a rage, emotions have won; logic is suppressed. When we act dispassionately, logic has won; emotions are suppressed. To review the seven choices outlined in Chapter 1 while a gunman holds a pistol to your head is to demonstrate a rare act of logic. To tell him what he wants to know unhesitatingly is to act emotionally. But even the most logical of us make some decisions emotionally, and the most emotional of us make some decisions logically. Which is the better decision, the one that arises from our *feelings* or the one that arises from our *reason?*

I know a young man who worked in the Arizona office of an international company. Several promotions had convinced him he was destined to rise to the top of the executive ladder. A logical analysis of his career objectives convinced him he should not spend much more time in the branch office. If he did, executive talent scouts might conclude that he could not play on Broadway.

"Honey," he said to his wife one evening, "how would you like to live in New York? That's the big time. That's where the action is."

"Live in New York!" said his wife. "You must be out of your mind. What about the filth and air pollution? The high cost of living? The noise and the crowds? When would I see Mother? Do you have any idea how much it would cost to pack up all our things and ship them to New York?"

So there it was: the classic case of the organization man ready to pack up and move to further his career. When the company says come, he cometh. When it says go, he goeth To object is to risk being on the list of nonpromotables, those who have placed their own concerns above their loyalty to the company. My friend, of course, had not yet received any orders, but he was going to do his best to generate them.

"If you go to New York," his wife continued, "you can go alone."

"Be logical, Bonnie," he said. "We wouldn't have to live in New York. We could get a nice place within commuting distance. There would be no crowds or air pollution. Don't worry about the cost of moving. The company would pick up the tab. We would see your mother on holidays, and think of all the museums and cultural advantages for the kids."

In spite of all Jim's arguments, the idea of moving to New York was inconceivable to his wife. "What about my job?" she said. "Do you know how many years I've put into teaching to get my tenure? Do you want me to throw all that away?"

Jim played what he considered to be his trump card. "If I could get a transfer to the New York home office, I would be in line for some really big money. We'd never miss your income."

It was the wrong thing to say. "Miss my income!" Bonnie shouted. "What about me missing my work?"

"You're a good teacher. You could get a good teaching job in New York, if you really wanted to, and it would probably pay you more than you get here."

Jim had a logical answer for everything. Bonnie maintained her misgivings but eventually agreed that he could ask for a transfer. Secretly she hoped that it would never come through.

But it did. Jim was jubilant. His career could now progress according to plan. Bonnie was dismayed at the news. Since she had given her reluctant approval to the transfer request, there was little more she could say. But she could cry. Through tears she said, "What you want always comes first. What I want comes second."

Jim tried to console her. "Don't you see? This is a terrific opportunity for both of us. You and the kids are the ones who are going to benefit most. If I make it, you make it. What's good for me is good for us."

In due course, Jim established his family in a fashionable New York suburb, with an impressively heavy mortage and a two-hour daily commute to work. He worked late, traveled on business extensively, and set himself a work schedule calculated to mash the fingers of any other young hopefuls with a grip on the promotional ladder.

It took about a year for Jim to face the fact that all was not well. He was aggravated and frustrated by the petty rivalries and office intrigues of company headquarters. He felt that people were looking over his shoulder, hoping he would stumble. His responsibility was greater in New York than in Arizona, but his freedom of action was more limited. And though he had made dozens of acquaintances, he wondered if he had found any real friends.

What brought his feelings to the surface was a picture on the desk of one of the company vice presidents. It showed his daughter in full riding costume, winning a prize at a horse show. "Hell," thought Jim, "do you have to be a vice president here to have your daughter ride a horse? We used to have horses in Arizona and never thought anything about it."

Jim found himself homesick for outdoor living, neighborhood barbecues, spectacular sunsets, and a job close to home. His wife and children missed their relatives, their old friends, and their informal lifestyle. In fact, they were miserable, and he was less than happy.

His decision to transfer to New York had been made in a perfectly logical way. He had found a reasonable answer to every objection Bonnie raised. Everything seemed to be going according to plan. He had received his promotion and a salary increase. He was successful in his work (the boss had said so). He had a beautiful home. The children were going to good schools.

What had he overlooked? Emotions and feelings, of course. Strictly speaking, Jim's analysis would have been more *logical* if he had anticipated the atmosphere he would face in New York and the effects of commuting and the change in lifestyle on himself and his family. But he had refused to let these "emotional" factors influence his decision.

There is no happy ending to the story of Jim and Bonnie. As of this writing, he is still plugging away in the New York office, and she is doing some substitute teaching. But both feel the move was a mistake.

Now consider the story of my wife's friend Shirley. Shirley dropped in at a neighbor's home just when the family had decided to send its unhousebroken collie pup to the dog pound. The pup stared up at her with big brown eyes and wagged his tail, turning her heart into melted butter. She took him home and adopted him.

At the end of three months certain changes had occurred in Shirley's life. She no longer sat in her favorite chair. The dog had taken a liking to it, not for sleeping but for chewing. When the dog was outside, he wanted to be inside. When he was inside, he wanted to be outside. When he was left alone, he barked for company. When he had company, he jumped on people's laps.

What had gone wrong? The melting effect of the soft brown eyes and the wagging tail made Shirley forget that neither she nor her husband had any experience with dogs. When Shirley made her decision to adopt, reason had not been consulted.

These stories demonstrate the importance of employing both reason and emotion in making decisions. Yet many of the books, articles, and business courses on decision making preach that "rational decision making" is the pinnacle we must all strive toward. We are told that when we enter the decision-making arena we must check our emotions outside, lest we be swayed by sentiment and diverted from our goals.

That's fine for a scientist conducting a laboratory experiment. But most of the decisions we make in life affect people, ourselves and others, and people by their very nature are beings who *feel* as well as *think*. A decision that reflects only logic may fail if those on whom its success depends reject it for emotional reasons. A decision we make for ourselves, no matter how logical, may not be right if it doesn't feel right. In my work, as in my own life, I have found that the most durable decisions are those that reflect both reason and emotion. *It is striking the right balance that is crucial.*

When we make a decision that affects others, we will have a much better chance of winning their acceptance and support if we consider their feelings. One of the principal causes of frustration in life is a feeling of powerlessness, which stems from an inability to make our voices heard. One of the chief sources of discontent in the world is the exclusion of great numbers of people from effective participation in the decisions that affect their lives. If the majority would let the minority in on more of the decisions, how many wars, riots, demonstrations, and murders might be prevented?

Forward-looking businesses give considerable thought to ways of accommodating the feelings of staff and workers. If a plant has to be closed down, how can it be done with the least amount of antagonism? If a new office is to be built, how can it be designed to provide a pleasant work atmosphere? What perquisites of rank can be provided to satisfy the status needs of people in the executive hierarchy?

Sometimes such perquisites have unintended effects. One corporation spent millions of dollars to build a campus-style headquarters in a fashionable suburb. Offices and desks had to be provided for thousands of people, from clerk to president. Obviously the accommodations could not be equal. Some offices had to be larger than others, some had to be furnished more elaborately than others; some had reception rooms, some did not. But an effort was made to insure that assistant directors in one division received the same accommodations as assistant directors in another division. Assistant directors, however, received more square footage than managers, and managers received more square footage than assistant managers. As ritualistic as the exercise may seem, leaders of this corporation insisted that it gave executives greater work incentive than would, say, a system of placing everyone in identical cubicles or in huge open rooms.

In the offices of assistant directors the company placed a rather expensive water carafe, with matching tray and tumblers. Twice a day a maintenance man traveled the corridors with a large demijohn of spring water mounted on a balloon-tied cart. He entered each assistant director's office, and refilled the carafe from the demijohn.

The assistant directors, of course, privately pooh-poohed the ceremony. They wanted everyone to know that they were not taken in by the attention displayed on their behalf. Being regular guys, they said they would have preferred to drink from the water fountains in the halls, but rather than cause a fuss they suffered the carafes.

Then the impossible happened. One of the managers, who was not entitled to a water carafe, saw an exact duplicate in a gift shop. He purchased it along with tray and tumblers and installed it on his desk. His superiors were outraged. Who was this upstart to infringe on the perquisite of the assistant directors? Did he have no consideration for their feelings? Was he a troublemaker? On the surface it looked like a tempest in a carafe. But thousands of dollars had been spent to provide symbols of achievement. If the system could be subverted by a rebellious maverick, what was the sense in setting up any system at all?

The unpleasant task of ordering the manager to remove the offensive carafe fell on the director of personnel administration. He had a heart-to-heart talk with the owner of the unauthorized carafe and eventually recommended its removal. But the manager's sales were up for that quarter. He was in no mood to back down without a fight. "I will not remove it," he said. "It is mine, I paid for it. Why shouldn't I keep it?"

The director of personnel administration consulted the assistant directors. Eventually the case was appealed to the general manager of the division. This astute executive did not throw the case out of court but took it under advisement. He knew the importance of taking feelings into account when he made a decision.

I was not his confidant and he was not my client. I have no way of knowing what went through his mind when the question was brought to him. However, I think I can reasonably reconstruct his thought process, as follows: "Do I have to make decisions about such trivia? Somebody's feelings will be hurt. Will that have an unfavorable impact on performance? Possibly. Since high performance is crucial, what should I do to protect it? If I rule that the carafe must be removed, will I lose a good sales manager? If I rule that it can remain, will the morale of the assistant directors suffer? What will be the consequences of that? I've got to protect everyone's feelings in order to protect performance."

After several days he announced his decision: the manager could keep the carafe, which was a victory for him, but it would no longer be filled from the demijohn, which was a victory for the assistant directors.

If anyone asked the manager how he fared in his confrontation with the director of personnel, he could truthfully say, "I stood up to him.

The company thinks so much of me that rather than fire me they let me keep my carafe." But after a few weeks the waterless carafe began to look a little silly on his desk. Of course, he could have filled it himself from the drinking fountain in the hall, but that would have been an indignity. Quietly he placed it on the bottom shelf of his bookcase, where it remained as a silent symbol of his victory and his defeat.

If anyone asked the assistant directors whether they were successful in defending their perquisite, they could truthfully say, "You don't see fresh spring water being served to managers anymore. In fact, you don't even see water carafes on managers' desks anymore, do you?"

If anyone asked the general manager how he settled the case of the celebrated carafe, he could truthfully say, "My team doesn't worry about carafes. All we concern ourselves with is performance."

Just as businesspeople accommodate the feelings of staff when making decisions that affect year-end earnings, so you should consider the feelings of family and friends when you make decisions that affect your personal life. But to what extent should emotion and feeling be consulted when you make a personal decision? When should one overrule the other? Should either predominate?

Thousands of men and women I have worked with have found this little figure, with or without the words, to be a useful guide in decision making. You may know it as the mathematical symbol for infinity. Right now, it will be useful for you to think of it as a pair of eyeglasses. One lens is the lens of feeling, the other the lens of thinking. (Later we'll develop some of its other uses.)

If you hold a finger in front of your nose and shut your right eye, your finger will jump to the right (where it really is not) and you will see partly around the finger on the right side. When you open both eyes you will see your finger in the center (where it really is) and be able to see partly around it from both sides. This is the well-known hemisphere test used to teach the concept of an optical illusion.

The finger that you see with both eyes is a truer representation of reality than the one you see with either eye alone. It has both depth and clarity. The decision that you make with the spectacles of feeling and thinking is a better decision than you can make with either emotion or logic alone. Like the one made by the general manager about the water carafe, it responds to the hard facts while recognizing human feelings. Effective decisions do both.

# 3

# The Pitfalls of Positive Thinking
# and Other Snares for the Unwary

In the absence of an organized body of knowledge about decision making, a kind of folklore has sprung up to fill the vacuum. Like an old-time medicine show, the folklore of decision making snares the unwary. It offers its own brand of snake oil as a cure for all ills. The snake oil of decision making comes in five bottles, labeled positive thinking, intuition, common sense, what-if, and pros and cons.

Many Americans have been trained to worship at the shrine of positive thinking. Rooting for a third-rate team is called school spirit by the principal. Boasting that Podunk is the best town in the state is called boosting by the chamber of commerce. Believing in an obsolete product is called self-confidence by the sales manager. It is no wonder that anyone who looks an unpleasant truth in the face and calls it to public attention risks being branded a troublemaker. But in order to make good decisions we have to learn to look unpleasant truths in the face.

The tires on your jalopy are so worn that it would take a braille expert to detect any tread. You have to make a long trip to visit relatives to keep peace in the family. The decision facing you is whether to do something about the tires now or wait until you come back. You would really like to spend your free cash on gas, motels, and meals, not tires. Should you take the positive attitude that everything will turn out all right if you leave home on the smooth treads? From this perspective, positive thinking is often nothing more than a disguise for wishful thinking.

More times than I like to remember, I have seen large corporations delude themselves by wishful thinking. The boss is under the gun to project a certain profit for the shareholders. He calls in a sales manager and says, "I've got your division down for $40 million this year and you've got to come up with it." The sales manager thinks, "I know I can't make it, but if I tell him so he'll think I'm a negative thinker. He likes positive thinkers. So I'll say I can make the $40 million and he can project his profits for the security analysts and, who knows, something may happen in the next 12 months. I'll use the time to scramble like hell and I'll send up plenty of flares so that when I don't make it he'll at least know I tried." The boss and the salesman are using wishful thinking to avoid facing reality.

Wishful thinking has no place in decision making. Positive thinking does, if you don't let it blind you to reality. Positive thinking may give you the motivation to turn a problem into an opportunity and transform adversity into advantage. In this sense, positive thinking means, not *assuming* the best, but always *seeking* the best while taking into account all the pitfalls that lie between your goals and their fulfillment.

Positive thinking can also increase your motivation to carry out a decision. You have decided to lose ten pounds for your school reunion. You don't want your old sweetheart to see you looking out of shape. Thinking positively about the day you will step on the scales may encourage you to run that extra mile or push away that strawberry sundae.

But if thinking positively prompts you to ignore reality, it is more likely to lead to a bad decision than a good one. Sometimes in government and business, ignoring reality is a kind of benign conspiracy. All the conspirators really know better, but because of previous commitments of energy and money they go on pretending that all is well, postponing the inevitable. A friend of mine calls this strategy "Save face now, lose face later."

A large machinery manufacturer desperately needed a new product line to boost its falling sales. The research department had developed an idea for a photocopying machine that would operate on an entirely new principle. "How soon can it be in production?" asked the president, anxious to reverse the sales trend. The question was relayed through the various levels of management. "Two years" was the reply from the bottom, but as the estimate was relayed back up the line, each layer of management trimmed a few months off the original estimate in order to make itself look good.

There still was no machine when the president, following the timetable he'd been given, announced he would visit the laboratory in a week to inspect the prototype. Working day and night, the staff managed to get one machine operating on the morning of the president's inspection. It worked beautifully for one cycle while he watched. As soon as he left, it caught on fire. Two weeks later a full-page ad in leading business publications announced the introduction of the new machine—at a time when the company did not even own an operating prototype!

What had gone wrong? There had been a conspiracy to ignore reality. Trying to please the president, who was trying to please the board of directors, who were trying to please the stockholders, the staff had been unable to tell the emperor he wasn't wearing any clothes.

Our government made a similar elaborate display of positive thinking during the war in Vietnam. Because of heavy commitments of troops, money, and emotion, the Pentagon was pressured to produce reports that all was going well. Officially inspired news leaks exaggerated Communist weaknesses while ignoring danger signs confronting our South Vietnamese allies. Similarly, for every soldier lost on our side, a larger number was reported lost on the enemy side. It was just a matter of time, U.S. leaders assured each other, until we would see "Light at the end of the tunnel." The result? We won the war on paper, but lost it on the field.

When you are making a decision for yourself, you are not likely to be part of a conspiracy to ignore reality, but you are in danger of falling prey to the snake oil of positive thinking. Use positive thinking *after* you have made your decision, not before.

Another snare for the unwary decision maker is intuition. Intuition is defined as quick perception of a truth without conscious attention or reasoning. Almost every family has a favorite story about intuition. The lady who told me this one swears it is true. Her grandfather, a successful New England industrialist, had taken the morning train from Ashland, New Hampshire, to Boston on business. While the train was stopped in the Nashua station, he had a sudden thought. "I think I'll change trains and go to Worcester to see Marjory." Marjory was his married daughter, who did not even live in Worcester.

On his arrival in Worcester, he took a cab to a local hospital, where he learned that Marjory had given birth an hour before to his first and only grandson. She had not known she would be rushed to the hospital that morning, and no one could have informed him after the fact because he was already on the train from Ashland before she left home. She regarded his presence as a miracle.

I asked the lady who told me the story whether Marjory had previously given birth to other children at the same hospital. She had. Did grandfather know this? He did. Were any of the other children

born earlier than the doctor had predicted? They were. Did grandfather know this? He did. Had he been informed of the predicted date
for the birth of the grandson? Probably. Thus, when grandfather sat in
the train at Nashua, could he not have calculated that if this child were
as early as the others, Marjory might be at the hospital in Worcester
right now? In fact, might he even have stepped off the train and
phoned the hospital to verify his intuition?

"You are just trying to spoil a good story," said my friend. "Besides,
grandfather was too much of a gentleman not to have told the whole
truth."

I have always believed, at the risk of spoiling good stories and losing
good friends, that what is called intuition is frequently based on
emotion or knowledge that is not always recalled at the moment. Good
poker players do not decide intuitively when to stay in the game and
when to drop out. They calculate the odds and pick up all the signs of
when their opponents are bluffing. The casual player may explain his
luck in terms of intuition. But did he really guess that Charlie was
bluffing when he stood pat? Or had he noticed that Charlie bites the
corner of his mouth when he is bluffing?

The brain tends to pick up a great deal of information without
knowing how it got there. Instead of blindly following your intuition
when you have a decision to make, you can use it constructively by
asking yourself the same kinds of questions I asked my friend about her
grandfather. Why do you intuitively feel that a certain course of action
is right? Did Charlie bite the corner of his mouth? Is there some fact or
bit of knowledge in your subconscious that should be included in the
conscious decision-making process? Do you lean toward a particular
decision because of a personal feeling? What is that feeling and why do
you have it? Get the answers to these questions out in the open and you
will be on your way to making a good decision, one that you can justify
to yourself and to others.

Justifying decisions is required more often in business and government than in personal life. You can frequently make a personal
decision based solely on intuition without justifying it. But the
president of a company who announces to his board of directors that
he has intuitively decided to build a new power plant may well be on
the road to involuntary retirement. He has to justify his decisions. Even
in your personal life, if you can support your decisions, they become
easier to live with and easier to explain to friends and family.

Another pitfall for the decision maker is so-called common sense.
Common sense usually produces decisions to do the obvious. You are
sitting at a bar when you are approached by a man who resembles a
gorilla. He has been celebrating. "Buddy," he snorts, "that's my chair

you are sitting in. You have five seconds to get out of it." You do not use the time to consider your civil rights or to reflect on the fact that his stomach is flabby while you have done 50 pushups this morning. Instead, you move over to the next chair. Common sense told you to.

The roof is leaking. You decide to patch it. Would it have been wiser to contract for a new roof or perhaps to sell the house? Neither of those courses would have kept you from getting wet today. It was only common sense to patch the roof. It was obvious.

But what if the decision you have to make has no obvious answer? How is common sense used or misused in making such a decision? A friend has asked you to be a partner in a fast-food franchise. Since you already have a job that meets the monthly mortgage payments and you have no experience in the food business, you politely reject the offer. It was only common sense, you say. But was it? Were you using common sense as an excuse for not thinking? Would it have been wiser to probe the feelings, thoughts, and experiences that comprise your common sense, just as you did with intuition? Perhaps if you had analyzed the offer on the basis of facts and feelings instead of common sense, you would be the owner of a successful fast-food franchise today.

Another snare for unwary decision makers is the what-if game. It can easily deceive people into believing they have done something extremely clever or foresighted. In its simplest form, a person sits down and tries to anticipate trouble by asking, "What if my kid, customer, boss, or competition does this or that? What should I do?"

The celebrated raconteur Ludwig Bemelmans tells the story of a maitre d'hotel who asked himself what if one of half a dozen flower girls with long dresses tripped on a step while carrying an elaborate wedding cake six feet in diameter. When one of the girls actually did trip and the cake was smashed to pieces to the horror of the wedding guests, the maitre d' merely clapped his hands twice. The lights went off briefly, the mess was cleaned up in the dark, and six standby flower girls entered through another door with a duplicate cake. The guests broke into applause. The maitre d' congratulated himself on his foresight.

In most situations, however, it is better to take *preventive* action and avoid mistakes than to wait for mistakes to occur and have to take *protective* or *reactive* action. Knowing of the danger of a slip, the maitre d' might have had the flower girls' dresses shortened or the steps eliminated.

The what-if game can be helpful if its primary purpose is preventive rather than reactive. It enables planners to take steps to reduce the likelihood of an undesirable event occurring while drafting contingency plans to cope with the worst if preventive action is unsuccessful.

Another pitfall for unwary decision makers—along with positive thinking, intuition, common sense, and what-if—is listing pros and cons. Suppose you are in the market for a house. The one you are seriously considering is well constructed, but the price is higher than you wanted to go. Still, it is in a quiet neighborhood and its value will appreciate; but it is far from your work. Still, the architecture is beautiful and there is a big yard for the kids; but it needs another bedroom.

You could go on juggling pros and cons like that forever, like a circus performer trying to keep a dozen plates spinning on the end of several long sticks. Just when he gets the ninth one spinning, he has to rush back to give the first another twirl. You get on this merry-go-round because you have no system for dealing with the list of pros and cons, for weighing their importance, and for making a decision you can have confidence in. Unless you are fortunate enough to find the impossible dream—the house with all advantages and no disadvantages—you could go around forever. If someone were to ask you to explain your decision to buy or not to buy the house, you could readily produce a laundry list of facts but not a conclusive justification.

Putting facts down on paper can be a useful tool, but there is a better way than merely listing pros and cons. My Seven Building Blocks will enable you to use positive thinking, intuition, common sense, and what-if constructively in an organized system of decision making and never again have to juggle pros and cons.

# Section II

## The Seven Building Blocks

# 4

# The Seven Building Blocks
# and What They Do

What is the purpose of a decision? A superficial answer is that a decision enables us to choose among two or more possible courses of action. But why make a choice at all? Basically, because we perceive a gap between what is happening—or may happen—and what we or someone else would like to see happen. There are several variations of this decision gap:

Something is wrong and needs to be corrected.
Something is threatening and needs to be prevented.
Something is inviting and needs to be accepted.
Something is missing and needs to be provided.

The decision-making process begins with the perception of this gap and ends with an action that will narrow or close it. Like a pie, the process of decision making can be sliced into any number of pieces. But the experience of thousands of business managers, using the techniques I have developed and refined, demonstrates that the easiest way to learn and use decision-making skills is to break them down into seven components. I call these the Seven Building Blocks. As we shall see, they are as applicable to personal problems as they are to business problems. The Seven Building Blocks are:

1. SMOKE OUT THE ISSUES: *Why is a decision necessary? What are the consequences of doing nothing?* (See Chapter 5.)

25

Answering these questions will tell you whether a decision is indeed called for and, if so, why. As we shall see in Chapter 5, many situations that appear to require a decision are found on further examination not to require any action at all. If the answers to these questions persuade you that a decision is necessary, proceed to Building Block No. 2.

2. STATE YOUR PURPOSE: *What needs to be determined? What do you want to decide? Why?* (See Chapter 6.)

Don't be satisfied with your first answers to these questions. Keep asking why until you have established your basic statement of Purpose. Try to state your Purpose as broadly as possible, rather than as an either/or proposition. In defining your Purpose, you may find it helpful to distinguish what the problem *is* from what it *is not*.

3. SET YOUR CRITERIA: *What do you want to achieve, preserve, and avoid by whatever decision you make?* (See Chapter 7.)

The answers to these questions become the standards or Criteria for evaluating possible courses of action.

4. ESTABLISH YOUR PRIORITIES: *What are the Criteria that any solution absolutely has to satisfy? What other Criteria should it meet?* (See Chapter 8.)*

The first group of Priorities are called *absolute requirements*, because no decision is acceptable unless it meets them. Lesser Priorities are labeled *desirable objectives* and are ranked in order of importance, from 10 (most desirable) downward.

5. SEARCH FOR SOLUTIONS: *How can you meet the Criteria you have set?* (See Chapter 9.)

List all the possible courses of action open to you and—here or in Building Block No. 6—gather any information that may be helpful in making a final selection.

6. TEST THE ALTERNATIVES: *How does each Alternative stack up against the Priorities?* (See Chapter 10.)

Does one emerge a clear winner? Does this "best" Solution have significant weaknesses in some areas? How can they be overcome? Consider combining features of two or more Alternatives to devise an even better decision. In adversary proceedings such as negotiations, refining your Alternatives to create an advantageous situation for all parties is often the key to a better decision.

---

*The importance of establishing priorities among Criteria and Alternatives has long been recognized by such authorities in the field as Norman Maier, Herbert Simon, Peter Drucker, Charles Kepner, Benjamin Tregoe, Irving Janis, and Leon Mann among others.

7. TROUBLESHOOT YOUR DECISION: *What could go wrong? How can your choice be improved?* (See Chapter 11.)
Create refinements that prevent, overcome, or minimize the dangers of the Alternative you select.

These are the Seven Building Blocks of creative decision making. They will be explored in the chapters that follow. Before considering them in detail, let's apply them to a problem to get a feel for how the process works. Study the following example carefully. In the world of decision making, process is paramount.

Not long ago Ernie, a young business associate of mine, was taking care of the affairs of an aunt who was confined to a private nursing home. He was trying to sell her house on Long Island, N.Y. He hoped the proceeds, invested in Triple A corporate bonds, together with her private pension and social security benefits, would meet the monthly bill for her care. A realtor had suggested asking $80,000 for the house but selling it for $75,000 if necessary. So far, the best offer had been $70,000, but it included a stipulation that my associate, as conservator, accept a personal mortgage on the house. What should he do?

In an effort to help him, I suggested that we work through the problem using the Seven Building Blocks. "If it'll help me do what's best, let's try it," said Ernie. We got out a scratch pad and went to work.

## 1. SMOKE OUT THE ISSUES: *Why is a decision necessary?*

"I know you're having trouble managing your aunt's affairs, and I hope everything will turn out well," I said. "But have you ever asked yourself why you're involved in her affairs at all?"

"Well," said Ernie, "I've accepted the legal responsibility of power of attorney, so I do have a fiduciary obligation toward my aunt. Besides, I feel a personal and moral responsibility to help her. If I did nothing, I'd feel rotten. You see, she has no one else."

"About the $70,000 offer," I said. "Why not forget it? Why do anything right now?"

"I don't know how much longer I can go on making up the deficit. My aunt's pension and social security don't cover the cost of her care. On top of that, the taxes and insurance on the house cost $400 a month. The taxes are going to go even higher. Since the house is unoccupied, it's a target for vandals. The garage has already been broken into. Selling would produce an income and get the responsibility off my back. To top it all off, I'm having trouble sleeping at night and my doctor says I'm worrying too much about the house."

"Then why not accept the offer?"

"The house is worth more than the offer, and if I take the mortgage the income won't be as much as good corporate bonds would yield."

I handed Ernie the pad I had been scribling on. It looked like this:

*Why is a decision necessary?*
You have a fiduciary responsibility toward your aunt.
You would feel bad if you did nothing.
You need additional money to maintain her health care.
It costs $400 a month *not* to sell her house.
Potential vandalism will reduce its value.
Taxes are climbing.
Responsibility for the house is a burden to you.

"It looks pretty complete to me," said Ernie. "Now what do we do with it?"

"Well," I replied, "let's look at the list from the perspective of Building Block No. 1. Do we have to make a decision?"

"I guess we do, for all the reasons you jotted down there."

I agreed and we went on to the next step.

2. STATE YOUR PURPOSE: *What needs to be determined?*

"I guess my Purpose is to sell my aunt's house," said Ernie, shrugging his shoulders.

At my suggestion, he wrote his tentative Purpose on the pad: "sell my aunt's house."

We continued the exercise. "Will you sell it at any price?" I asked.

"No, at fair market value, a minimum of $75,000."

"Why?"

"So I can get out from under the $400 a month and invest the proceeds to make up the deficit in her monthly payment."

"Why?"

"So that my aunt will be properly taken care of for the rest of her life."

"Okay," I said. "Let's try to distinguish what your Purpose *is* from what your Purpose *is not*. At this point, what do you think the Purpose is?"

"Well, I suppose it's to determine the best way to use her house to insure that she continues to have superior health care."

"It's not to sell the house?" I asked.

"No, that's just one possibility, but a strong one."

"It's not to get top dollar for the house?"

"No. Top dollar would be nice, but all I have to do is make sure my aunt has an income that will keep her in the rest home she's in now, or one that's as good."

"Quick, Ernie," I said, "write down your Purpose."

After hesitating a moment, Ernie produced the following statement of Purpose: "determine the best way to use my aunt's house to finance her health care."

3. SET YOUR CRITERIA: *What do you want to achieve, preserve, and avoid by whatever decision you make?*

"You know my methods, Ernie," I said. "I don't solve your problems. I give you a process—a compass—to guide your search for a Solution. Now what do you want to *achieve, preserve,* and *avoid* by whatever you decide to do about your aunt's house?"

"Well, I want to be able to feel I've fulfilled my obligations, both legal and moral. She is short $550 a month right now. I need to find a way to provide that money for the rest of her life."

"Write those down under *achieve.* But don't forget that you want to be able to sleep nights again too. You couldn't, for instance, produce the $550 by investing your aunt's assets in soft-drink vending machines that you'd have to service."

Ernie jotted down several things. "I'm working on what I have to *preserve* now. I know I want to preserve my aunt's residence in the rest home and preserve the equity in her house for her benefit. I'm trying to think if there's anything else."

"Good," I said. "But haven't you overlooked the fact that during the five months you've had the house for sale you've already watched the equity erode by $2,000? I figure that's what the taxes and insurance have cost you so far."

"It's worse than that. To keep the plumbing—and the prospective buyers—from freezing, I've had to keep the heat on. And you and I both know how the price of fuel oil has skyrocketed lately."

"So there's one more thing you have to *achieve.* You have to minimize the time it takes to do something about the house. What's the longest you can hold out?"

"It's been too long already. Another two months would be the outside limit."

"Put that down. Now let's consider what you have to *avoid,* and then let's take a look at your list."

"Well, even though I'm under pressure, I want to avoid selling at a distress price. I want to avoid excessive fees for realtors and lawyers, and of course I want to avoid vandalism."

When Ernie got through writing, he presented me with this list:

## PURPOSE

Determine the best way to use my aunt's house to finance her health care

## CRITERIA

Achieve
  A feeling of having fulfilled my responsibility
  An additional $550 monthly for the rest of my aunt's life
  Freedom from worry about the house
  Freedom from excessive responsibility for any investment
  Minimum risk in any investment or Solution
  Quick action (two-month limit)

Preserve
  My aunt's continued residence in the rest home or its equivalent
  The current equity in her house

Avoid
  Selling at a distress price that would not produce sufficient income for my
    aunt's care
  Vandalism
  Excessive professional fees

"That's a pretty good list, Ernie, but in this world you don't usually get everything you want. Shakespeare didn't want to, but he wrote some flops. Babe Ruth didn't want to, but he struck out now and then."

"I can see what's coming," said Ernie. "You're now talking about setting Priorities."

"Right," I said. "We're talking about going on to Building Block No. 4. Before we do, though, do you remember what the first three were?"

"Well, first we had to decide if we needed a decision at all, so No. 1 was smoking out the Issues: 'Why is a decision necessary?'"

"Very good."

"No. 2 was a statement of Purpose: 'What are we trying to determine?' And I remember that the more we probed our tentative statement, the broader our Purpose became. We thought first the Purpose was to sell my aunt's house, but we ended up deciding it was to determine the best way to use it."

"And No. 3?"

"That was setting our Criteria, listing what we wanted to *achieve*, *preserve*, and *avoid* by any decision we made."

"Excellent, Ernie. Now let's see how important all those Criteria you jotted down are."

4. ESTABLISH YOUR PRIORITIES: *What are the Criteria that any Solution absolutely has to satisfy? What other Criteria should it meet?*

"Are there some things on your list," I asked, "that are essential and some that are only desirable?"

"Only two things are really essential. One is to obtain the $550 monthly and the other is to keep my aunt in that rest home or a comparable one. The first makes the second possible."

"Suppose the most you could get from the house was $500 a month? Could you manage?" I asked.

"I suppose I could make up the difference."

"Then the $550 a month is not essential, but $500 a month is. Or, to use my terminology, $500 a month is an *absolute requirement;* anything more than that is a *desirable objective.* Place a star beside your two absolutes and then take a hard look at all the other items on your list. How important are they on a scale of 10 (the highest) to 1? Maybe if you can get your two absolutes, the others won't be as important as you thought."

Here is Ernie's revised list of Criteria, with values assigned to the desirable objectives:

## PURPOSE

Determine the best way to use my aunt's house to finance her health care

## CRITERIA

Absolute Requirements
   Continue aunt in rest home
   Obtain $500 monthly from the house

Desirable Objectives
  10  Minimum risk in any investment or Solution
   9  Quick action (within two months, if possible)
   8  Preservation of current equity in her house
   8  More than $500 monthly for the rest of her life ($550 if possible)
   7  A feeling of having fulfilled my responsibility
   7  Avoid selling at a distress price that would not produce sufficient income for my aunt's care
   6  Freedom from worry about the house
   6  Freedom from excessive responsibility for any investment
   5  Avoid vandalism
   4  Minimum professional fees

"Okay," I said, "now let's review the list. Are there any objectives that the Solution absolutely has to satisfy?"

"Just two," Ernie concluded. "I could live with worrying about the house and continued vandalism, I suppose, and all the others that we called desirable objectives, but we have to find a way to get $500 a month out of the house and keep my aunt in her rest home. I guess that's why they're absolute requirements and the others aren't."

"Exactly," I said. "You learn fast."

5. SEARCH FOR SOLUTIONS: *How can you meet the Criteria you have set?*

"How many courses of action are open to you now, Ernie?" I asked.

"Well, I could accept the $70,000 offer or reject it and wait for a better one. That makes two."

"That's true," I said, "but remember that old Jack Benny routine where the robber sticks a gun in his ribs."

"Yes, what about it?"

"Well, the thug says, 'Which will it be, mister, your money or your life?' And Benny answers, 'I'm thinking it over.' Benny hesitated because he was a skinflint. He couldn't decide which of the two was more important. A choice that seems obvious to you and me wasn't obvious to him. He questioned it. Maybe you should question your choices too. There may be more Alternatives than at first meet the eye."

"Such as?"

"You try to think of some," I said. "Think about what you want to *achieve, preserve,* and *avoid.* Think about your Purpose—to use your aunt's house to finance the level of health care she needs. What ways can you think of to fulfill it? List them all, no matter how improbable they appear. Nothing is barred right now. Later we'll study them and get the information we need to decide how well they meet your Criteria."

Ernie worked for a few minutes and handed me his list.

"Good," I said, "but haven't you overlooked at least two possibilities: donating the house to a charitable institution in return for an annuity and investigating government assistance for your aunt?"

He made the additions, then gave me this list of Alternatives:

## POSSIBLE SOLUTIONS
Accepting the $70,000 offer and taking the mortgage
Rejecting the offer and waiting for a better one

Making a counteroffer
Renting the house
Moving into the house myself and applying my present rent money to my
    aunt's bills
Donating the house to a charitable institution in return for an annuity
Investigating government assistance for my aunt

"Well, Ernie, you've increased your possibilities from two to seven.
Good work."
"Yes," he said, "but how realistic are they all?"
"That's what we have to explore now."

## 6. TEST THE ALTERNATIVES: *How does each Alternative stack up against the Priorities?*

"Building Block No. 6 measures the possible solutions against our
Priorities," I said. I showed Ernie how to prepare a table to test his
Alternatives. It looked like Chart A, shown on the next page.
When the table was completed, I said, "It appears to me that you
lack a lot of the information you need to make a wise decision, but
that's all right. One of the purposes of testing is to show you where you
need to develop data. About this counteroffer, you're certainly going to
have to find out more about the prospective buyer before you can make
one."
"I don't see much chance of getting him to go higher," Ernie replied.
"You see, he has already come up from $66,000 to $70,000."
"Why does he want you to take the mortgage? Why doesn't he get a
bank mortgage?"
"I don't know," said Ernie.
"Well, if you're going to get the information you need, you can begin
by calling the realtor."
Ernie came back into my office a few minutes later, looking
dejected. "It doesn't look good," he said. "The buyer is a freelance
journalist and photographer with two children. He says he makes good
money, but the realtor suspects he wants me to take the mortgage
because banks don't like to make loans to people without steady jobs.
He is short on cash. He made the low offer so that he would have some
money left to modernize the house and put in a new kitchen. My aunt
never spent a dime on the kitchen."
"How much money are we talking about for improvements?" I
asked.
"When he made his first offer of $66,000, he offered a $10,000
downpayment. When he came up $4,000 to $70,000, he raised his
downpayment offer by the same $4,000. He's not apt to go any higher,

v = value    **CHART A**       **Purpose: Determine the best way to use my aunt's house to finance her health care**

| CRITERIA | ALTERNATIVE A Accept $70,000 Offer | ALTERNATIVE B Reject $70,000 Offer | ALTERNATIVE C Make Counter-offer | ALTERNATIVE D Rent House | ALTERNATIVE E Move in Myself | ALTERNATIVE F Donate House for Annuity | ALTERNATIVE G Seek Government Assistance |
|---|---|---|---|---|---|---|---|
| **Absolute Requirements** | | | | | | | |
| Aunt's continued residence in rest home | Possibly | Possibly | Don't know; need data | Temporarily | Yes | Don't know; need data | Don't know; need data |
| $500 extra monthly | Yes | Unknown | Don't know; need data | Temporarily | No | Don't know; need data | Don't know; need data |
| **V Desirable Objectives** | | | | | | | |
| 10 Minimum risk to assets | Don't know; need data | Some risk | Don't know; need data | Don't know; need data | ✕ | Yes | Yes |
| 9 Quick action | Yes | No | Don't know; need data | Don't know; need data | | Doubtful | Doubtful |
| 8 More than $500 extra monthly | No | Unknown | Don't know; need data | Temporarily | | Don't know; need data | Don't know; need data |
| 8 Preservation of equity | Partially | Erodes at $500 a month | Possibly | Don't know; need data | | Don't know; need data | Yes |
| 7 A feeling of having fulfilled responsibility | No | Possibly | Partially | Yes | | Don't know; need data | No |
| 7 Avoid selling at distress price | No | Possibly | Possibly | Yes | | Yes | Yes |
| 6 Freedom from worry about house | Yes | Not at present | Don't know; need data | No | | Yes | Yes |
| 6 Freedom from investment responsibilities | Yes | No | ? | No | | Yes | No |
| 5 Avoid vandalism | Yes | Increases exposure | Possibly | Yes | | Yes | Yes |
| 4 Minimum professional fees | Don't know; need data | Possibly | Don't know; need data | Yes | | Yes | Yes |

because then he wouldn't have enough cash left to make the necessary improvements."

"Let's go to lunch," I said.

Seated in a restaurant, nibbling on Greek olives, I said, "Ernie, do you remember when I left for that business conference in Detroit? One of the visual aids I took with me was that mathematical symbol that looks like a double lens. In each lens we had written the word 'win.' It's a reminder that in negotiations you have a much better chance of striking a deal if both parties win. If this freelance journalist gave you $75,000 for your aunt's house, you'd win and he would lose. If you accepted his $70,000 offer, he'd win and you would lose. Let's find a way you both can win."

"Do you mean we should split the difference?"

"No. What I mean is that he probably can't get a mortgage from a bank. That means there are very few houses he can purchase. He would like to have your aunt's. He is also strapped for cash to modernize the house, but he wants it so badly he has already agreed to take $4,000 of his improvement money to increase the downpayment. That means he is going to have to skimp and delay on improvements, a plan his wife probably won't like very much. What would it take to make him a winner?"

"A mortgage and $4,000 extra in his pocket to make improvements."

"What would it take to make you a winner?"

"The $75,000 and a quick sale."

"Well?"

"I'll call the realtor back and tell him I'll take the mortgage and reduce the downpayment by $4,000 if the prospective buyer will come up to $75,000. Since he is making good money, he'll barely notice the difference in the monthly payments for the increased mortgage. Besides, they are deductible. He'll *win* and I'll *win*."

"Hold on now," I said. "Haven't you overlooked something?"

"What's that?"

"What if something goes wrong?" I replied. "Remember our final Building Block?"

Ernie looked puzzled, so I repeated it for him.

7. TROUBLESHOOT YOUR DECISION: *What could go wrong?*

Ernie thought a moment. "I don't really know what could go wrong," he confessed.

"Well, let's look at your Criteria again. One was a minimum-risk investment. Now, selling a $75,000 house to a man without a steady job is not a risk-free deal if you hold the mortgage."

"When you look at it that way, I guess not."

"For example," I continued, "suppose your buyer defaults after a month or two and you have to foreclose on the house and sell it again. The lawyer and realtor fees would be doubled and you'd again have to put out $400 a month, maybe more by then, for taxes and insurance. Avoiding excessive professional fees and preserving the equity in the house were also on your list of Criteria. Have they suddenly become so unimportant that you're willing to ignore them? If so, why did you rate them so highly?"

"But what can I do?"

"Do what you are doing now. Tailor your counteroffer to satisfy your Criteria."

Ernie came up with the idea of running a professional credit check on his buyer while the buyer ran a title search on the house. If the sale fell through because of a defect in the title, the buyer's deposit would be returned. But if the sale fell through because Ernie found the credit report unsatisfactory, the expenses of the credit report would be deducted before the deposit was returned.

"Suppose he does have a good credit record," I said, "but through no fault of his own he is still unable to meet the payments. The money would not be coming in for your aunt and you would have the extra expense of reselling. What is the realtor's commission?"

"Six percent. On a sale of $75,000 it comes to $4,500. If I have to foreclose and resell, it would be $9,000."

"What can you do to minimize the risk?"

Ernie pondered and then spoke tentatively. "If, after the journalist moves in, he puts in a new kitchen and makes other improvements, the house will be worth more than it is right now. I believe he would modernize, because a family with children couldn't live in the house the way my aunt left it. Then if I had to foreclose, I might get a better price on a second sale. But with the time lag and the extra commission I would probably still suffer a loss. Maybe I can get the realtor to reduce his commission if he has to sell the house a second time."

"Put your win/win spectacles back on again, Ernie. This time it's you and the realtor who have to win. The buyer is not concerned. What does the realtor want?"

"He wants to earn a commission for both sales."

"What do you want?"

"A reduction in the commission on the second sale, if any. I have to preserve the equity."

"What guarantees does he have that you would even do business with him on a second sale?" I asked.

"I'll make it a condition of the first sale that he gets exclusive right of resale if there is a foreclosure."

"Suppose he were to agree to a reduced commission on the second sale, collect his full commission on the first sale, and then not try very hard to sell the house the second time because of his reduced commission. You would have to get another realtor at full commission."

"I could ask for my reduction on the first sale and pay full commission on the second sale," said Ernie.

"Suppose there is no second sale. Remember, you want to make him a winner."

"I've got it. I'll pay him half his commission for the first sale on closing and put the other half in escrow. If there is no mortgage default within a year, he'll get his money with interest. If there is a default, he'll waive the amount in escrow but still get full commission on the second sale. So if there is no foreclosure, he gets both halves of his commission, plus interest, but it will take a year. And if there is a foreclosure, he gets three halves. There's no way he can lose."

"Ernie," I said, "you're ingenious."

He smiled. "I know it, but do you think he'll agree to these terms?"

"What does he have for his work right now?"

"Nothing. In fact, he is out of pocket for the advertising."

"I think he'll agree."

When we got back to the office, Ernie called the realtor to make his counteroffer. He was promised an answer within 24 hours.

The next day when he came into my office he was jubilant. "The realtor called me at home last night. He couldn't wait 24 hours. Both he and the journalist agreed to everything we worked out at lunch yesterday. I'll get $75,000 for the house, the journalist will get his mortgage and new kitchen, and the broker will get his commission. Everybody wins."

"Sounds great," I said. "But just to check, let's test this Solution against your Criteria. Will it meet your two absolutes?"

"Yes. The realtor worked out the monthly payments for me last night. The mortgage payments and the yield on the downpayment will amount to even more than the $550 we put down as desirable. The mortgage runs for 25 years. It's just as though my aunt had purchased an annuity. So she is a winner too. I have preserved the equity, put an end to the fear of vandalism, avoided selling at a distress price, minimized the risk and the professional fees, and gotten the responsibility off my neck."

"You still have six more possible Solutions to test against your Criteria. Perhaps one of them will be even better."

He stared at me. "Haven't *you* overlooked something?"

"What's that?"

"One of my Criteria is to do something about the house as quickly as possible. It will take a lot of time to develop data on the other Solutions, especially the one about moving into the house myself. The journalist, on the other hand, is willing to sign the sales agreement and give me $2,000 deposit tomorrow."

"So you rule out the other Solutions because they don't meet the time requirement?"

"I throw into the balance that time costs me $400 or more a month, that its passage increases the possibility of vandalism and jeopardizes the sale to the journalist. Quick action rated a 9 on my list of Criteria." He paused, smiled, and said, "Besides, I don't feel like moving to New York to live in my aunt's house and I don't feel like looking for another job. I like it here."

"Then your decision satisfies your feelings as well as your thinking?"

He stared at me again. "John," he said, "your method is as important to you as my Solution is to me, isn't it?"

"Of course," I said. "The method helped you think your problem through. It clarified your Criteria and widened your search for Solutions. It showed you that $500 a month was sufficient to keep your aunt in the rest home. If you'd found a way merely to do that, you probably would have been satisfied. But what happened is that this particular system of decision making released your creativity. It forced you to train your mental searchlight in corners where you never would have ventured. And in one of those corners you found a truly innovative Solution to your problems."

The story of Ernie and his aunt's house is true. I did not concoct it just to explain the Seven Building Blocks. The house was sold on the terms Ernie developed. The realtor, who had been in the business 40 years, commented: "I thought I had seen everything, but this was a new one to me." When he gave a speech before a group of realtors, he used Ernie's counteroffer as a creative case history. To this day, he does not know he was on the receiving end of the Seven Building Blocks.

Innovative Solutions are characteristic of the Seven Building Blocks. Some people, of course, are more creative than others, but experience suggests that most people have more creativity than they suspect. ExecuTrak helps bring it out. It doesn't give you what you don't have. But it helps maximize what you do.

Remember the seven steps by asking yourself these questions:

| Question | Building Block |
|----------|----------------|
| Why | 1. is a decision necessary? SMOKE OUT THE ISSUES |

| Question | Building Block |
|----------|----------------|
| | 2. am I trying to determine? STATE YOUR PURPOSE |
| What | 3. do I want to achieve, preserve, and avoid? SET YOUR CRITERIA |
| | 4. criteria are essential or absolute and what criteria are only desirable? ESTABLISH YOUR PRIORITIES |
| How | 5. can I meet the criteria? SEARCH FOR SOLUTIONS |
| | 6. does each Alternative stack up? TEST THE ALTERNATIVES |
| What | 7. could go wrong? TROUBLESHOOT YOUR DECISION |

To help remember the sequence, I sometimes think of these as the *Why Would Howard?* (why/what/how/what) questions.

Knowing what the Seven Building Blocks are is merely an introduction. Discovering how to make them work for you is the subject of the next seven chapters.

# 5

## Building Block No. 1: Smoke Out the Issues

The need for a decision presupposes the existence of a problem. To make a good decision, you must first have a complete understanding of the problem. How do you get that kind of understanding? By asking yourself three questions:

1. *Why?* . . . *Why?*
2. What *is/is not* the problem?
3. What *is/should be/could be* happening?

These three steps are a tool kit to help you define the problem and assess the need for action. You should always ask question 1 and either question 2 or 3 (sometimes both). Whatever the situation, the tool kit will make the problem visible—if indeed there is a problem at all. The case histories in this chapter are designed to give you a feel for the power of these three tools at work. If you submit some problem of your own to the same tests, the process will become part of your own thinking.

1. *Why?* . . . *Why?*
Why do anything? Why not forget the whole thing and go fishing? Sometimes "going fishing" is the best answer.

An elderly lady who rented out her summer cottage became disturbed at summer's end when she received an intemperate note from the vacating family. The note detailed a number of alleged deficiencies in the cottage, demanded that it be cleaned and repaired, and insisted it had not been worth the rent she had charged. Not accustomed to such criticism, the lady began considering ways of placating the family. Should she write an apology? Offer to refund a portion of the rent? Make repairs? Hire a cleaning service?

I asked her to let me see the note. "Why, it's full of insults," I said, a bit startled that someone would use such language in addressing an elderly lady. Then I crumpled up the note and tossed it in her wastebasket.

"Why did you do that?"
"You clean and repair the cottage every spring, don't you?" I asked.
"Yes."
"You spend a week in the cottage yourself in July?"
"Yes."
"You have never received any complaints from other tenants?"
"No."
"You have a waiting list of prospective tenants?"

"Yes."
"They pay good rent?"
"Yes."
"Then you have no decision whatever to make."

The lady had no decision to make because nothing undesirable would happen if she did absolutely nothing. No harm would come to her values, her cottage, or her income. She was satisfied in her own mind that she was giving value for the money and that the cottage was in decent condition; no other tenants had ever complained. Consequently, no action was the right action. The reason? There would be no undesirable consequence from doing nothing.

Most of the time you won't get off as easily as the lady with the cottage. Asking *why* any decision is necessary often produces a list of possible consequences and conditions, some of them unpleasant or undesirable. The Purpose of your decision is to reduce, remove, or prevent the unpleasantness. Under these circumstances, telling yourself no action is needed may only aggravate the problem.

In direct contrast to the lady who thought she had a problem when she didn't, the manager of a factory thought he had no problem when he really had a serious one. The custom in this Louisville, Kentucky, factory was for the hourly help, mostly female, to bring in fresh-cut flowers every morning to make the plant a more pleasant place to work in. The workers did not buy the flowers. They grew them in their own gardens. Bringing them in for display had become a tradition. It was a good one. It prompted the workers to praise each other for their horticultural accomplishments and helped engender good morale.

Suddenly one morning no one brought flowers to the factory. Management didn't notice. For an entire week the plant suffered a drab, flowerless existence. At the end of the week, at a regular superintendents' meeting, the plant manager casually remarked, "Gee, what happened to all the flowers around here?" The superintendents did not know, but they soon found out. The hourly help was unhappy with the change in shift hours. They had chosen protest of the mildest possible form: withholding the flowers.

At the next meeting the general manager was informed of the source of concern. What should be done? "We'll let it ride and see what happens," he said and went on to other business. A few days later, frustrated that their mild protest had been ignored, the workers resorted to a costly wildcat strike.

Obviously, if the manager had asked why a decision was necessary, he would have concluded that taking no action could have unpleasant consequences; and those consequences were costly enough for him to consider preventive action. In choosing to do nothing, he made a decision by default—the wrong decision.

Recognizing a problem and asking, "Why is a decision necessary?" is an important technique in problem solving and decision making. It's the first step in smoking out the Issues. But say you've decided that a decision is necessary. What do you do next? Don't accept your first answer. Keep questioning each answer as often as necessary to smoke out the Issues. Ask *why* until the Issues—for you—are exhausted.

Suppose your problem is deciding whether to get some new living room furniture. *Why?* Because your daughter is ashamed to entertain her friends at home. You should not accept that answer without again asking why. *Why* is she ashamed to entertain her friends? Is it because of the furniture or is it because she doesn't want you to see her friends? You may have a daughter problem, not a furniture problem.

Suppose your problem is a teacher's complaint that Johnny is getting poor grades. *Why?* Because he is coming to class unprepared. *Why?* Because he isn't doing his homework. *Why?* Because he doesn't have a place to study. You may have a furniture problem, not a son problem.

It is very easy to deceive yourself with superficial answers. By asking why repeatedly—and verifying the answers—you can peel your way down to the *real* issue. When the *real* issue is finally exposed, you will be in a better position to make a correct decision. Don't be concerned if, as you keep asking why, the problem seems to enlarge. The range of possible solutions will also enlarge. My friend Ernie, you remember, thought that his problem was deciding whether to accept an offer for his aunt's house. It turned out that it really was how best to use his aunt's assets to keep her in the rest home.

Asking why is a continual process. The answers we generate today may be valid, but changing conditions can render them invalid tomorrow. If we are wrapped up in a cocoon of habit, we may continue to do things a certain way when there is no longer justification for doing so. We need to constantly examine our reasons to see whether they are still sound and whether we still remember them.

One Navy warship had a tradition of anchoring with the port anchor. The reason had long been forgotten. When a new captain was assigned to the ship, he wondered why the port anchor was always used. Coming into an anchorage one afternoon, he gave the order, "Stand by the starboard anchor!" Preparations were made. When the ship had reached the correct bearing the captain ordered, "Let go the starboard anchor!" There was a rumbling in the hawsepipe as the chain payed out, followed by a satisfactory splash. Then, to the amazement of the captain, the starboard anchor drifted slowly away from the ship. Stunned sailors lined the rail. A grizzled bo's'n's mate swore, "I'll be damned, the thing floats!"

The reason for anchoring with the port anchor was that the starboard anchor was made of wood. A previous captain had lost the original iron starboard anchor by trying to anchor in water that was too deep. Reporting his error would have ruined his career. A kindly old ship's carpenter had said, "Don't worry, cap'n. I know where I can get a couple of old railroad ties that I can carve to make you another anchor. When I paint it gray and pull it up in the hawsepipe, no one will ever be able to tell it from the real thing." With the change in ship's company through the years, the wooden anchor had been forgotten, but the custom of using the port anchor survived.

When we make decisions, it is important to remember our reasons for them and to make sure they are still valid. If they are not, we must generate new ones. *Why?* . . . *Why?* gives us the reasons.

### 2. *Is/is not*

The answers to "Why is a decision necessary?" usually come easily when we are dealing with facts. But many decisions involve emotions and attitudes. Being human, we have frailties. If we refuse to admit certain things to ourselves, we may not answer our own questions truthfully. We expect the psychological mirror on the wall to tell us that indeed we are the fairest of them all. When we begin to suspect the reflection we see in the psychological mirror is not a true one, the *is/is not* tool is especially effective. We must ask ourselves. "What *is* the problem? What *is not* the problem?" and, by so doing, winnow it down to its core.

A neighbor of mine asked me to help his daughter make a decision. She was a bright girl in her senior year at a state university. She had already received acceptances from two out-of-state law schools. Was her problem deciding which one to accept? Not at all. It seems girl met boy. Boy was pressing girl to marry him. He was a law student too, but he was attending school in their home state. Since it was too late for her to apply to his school, marriage would mean no law school for her next year. Going to an out-of-state law school would mean no marriage for her for at least a year.

"She is better at making up her face than making up her mind," said her father. "Her emotions are pulling her in one direction and her brains in another. I wish you could find time to talk to her."

Julie had it all: looks, personality, brains. Tossing her hair, she quickly whizzed through the reasons for making any decision. If she made no decision at all and "just went fishing," she would lose both a husband and a law career.

"Let's try *is/is not,* Julie," I said. "Is the problem that Barry doesn't love you?"

"No, he loves me." (*is not*)

"Is the problem that you don't love him?"

"No, I love him." (*is not*)

"Is the problem that you feel that law school will be too tough for you?"

"No, I know it will be a challenge, but I like challenges." (*is not*)

"Is the problem that Barry won't be able to hack it in his second year of law school?"

"No. He's not a genius, but he'll hack it." (*is not*)

On we went, separating fact from fiction as Julie saw it. "Is the problem that you might be a better lawyer than Barry?"

"No. Even if that were so, I think Barry could stand it." (*is not*)

"Is the problem that marrying Barry means postponing law school?"

"Yes, that really worries me." (*is*)

"Aha," I said, "now we're getting somewhere. What is it that worries you about postponing law school?"

"I'm not sure," Julie said, puzzled. Then she gulped and blurted it out. "If we get married now, there won't be enough money for both of us to go to law school. Since he's already started, I'd end up taking a job to pay the bills. I might get pregnant, and while he was trying cases I'd be burping babies. He would be changing venues and I'd be changing diapers. Even if I didn't have a baby, I'd have to work to support us for several years."

"It's not just postponing law school that bothers you then?" I said.

"No. The problem really is that if I marry Barry now, I'm afraid I'll never have a law career." (*is*)

Her words hung in the air. Her lips trembled. "Why doesn't he see that I'm trying to do what is best for both of us? Why doesn't he help me? If he loves me," she said, "why does he do this to me?"

Julie had discovered that marriage to Barry now might mean the end of her law career. The *real* issue had been smoked out.

Asking what the problem *is not*, by the process of elimination, can help uncover a truth that we may have been hiding from ourselves. Julie is now attending law school at an out-of-state university and getting good grades. She and Barry see each other on holidays, but they have no definite plans. My feeling is that if there's going to be a marriage in the future, Julie will be the one who decides.

Before moving on, let's review the process Julie and I used to smoke out her real problem. "Why is a decision necessary?" Because, Julie said, if she did nothing, she would lose both a husband and a law career. "What *is/is not* the problem?" Playing this game forced her to face up to the real issue—the potential loss of her career.

Sometimes we try to sweep a real problem under the rug. We try to pretend the problem isn't there, because the truth would be too awful to contemplate. Running away from *is/is not* may postpone a difficulty but will probably aggravate it in the long run. The sooner the truth is faced, the quicker corrective action can be taken and the less trauma there will be.

The president of a well-known firm of consulting engineers, normally a cool, detached individual, was not above sweeping a problem under the rug. His failure to use *is/is not* caused his company to suffer a 25 percent turnover in professional staff at a time when it needed experienced consultants because of an expansion program.

The president had noticed that one of his most capable young executives, who had just opened up the overseas division, was not happy. The young man had tried to talk to him about the changing nature of the firm, but the president became uncomfortable at such times and quickly cut him off. Without making any attempt to find out the real problem, he fabricated his own version and Solution. One morning he called the young man into his office and, after the ritual of coffee, launched into a little speech.

"I've been meaning to talk to you for some time," he said. "I've noticed that you look unhappy and seem quite preoccupied. So far, nobody has observed any effect on your performance, but I am certainly concerned. To show our appreciation for your fine work and to express our confidence in your future, even though you received a 15 percent merit increase only five months ago, effective next month you are getting another 10 percent increase. I hope this shows our faith in you and demonstrates to your wife that we appreciate how difficult it must be to raise young children with you traveling so much and working so hard."

The young man was shocked. He had been hoping for a chance to tell the boss what was really troubling him. It was not that he was overworked or that his wife had been complaining about his absence. It was that as the firm had grown it had lost its original character and innovativeness. Some of the individuals who were moving into upper management were more qualified to be Madison Avenue hucksters than consulting engineers. But the young man said nothing.

If the president had used *is/is not*, the conversation might have gone like this:

"Is the problem that you are working too hard?"

"No. I'm working hard but it's no problem." (*is not*)

"Is the problem that you are away from home too much?"

"No. I'm away from home, but my wife understands and knows it is only temporary." (*is not*)

"Is the problem that we haven't rewarded you financially for the good work you've done?"

"No. You have been very fair." (*is not*)

"Is the problem that the nature of your work has been changing as the company has grown?"

"No. It is that the nature of the company has been changing as my work has grown." (*is*)

Instead of smoking out the Issues, the president in effect used the salary increase to buy silence. In trying to purchase a yes-man, he cut off the very source that could have told him what the problem was. Not knowing—or knowing and refusing to face—the facts, the president was in no position to take corrective action.

Three months later the young man met the president's flight from Europe at Kennedy Airport. He announced that he was leaving the company. During the next *two* years the company suffered a 60 percent turnover in its professional staff.

*Is/is not* is a powerful tool. If the president had used it, he might have kept his rising young star and headed off the disastrous turnover in his staff.

### 3. *Is/should be/could be*

The third tool that helps us smoke out the Issues is a supplement to—and sometimes a substitute for—the second. Asking "What *is*? What *should be*? What *could be*?" forces us to face up to the differences between reality, expectation, and desire or conceivability.

Let's look first at reality. If you were to plot your life on a graph to depict what *is* happening, the vertical dimension would measure how you feel about your performance in life; the horizontal, the passage of time.

The peaks might include catching a winning football pass in a crucial high school game, getting into the college of your choice, landing a coveted job, vacationing in Acapulco, and getting married. The valleys might include getting jilted by an old flame, spending six weeks in bed with pneumonia, wrecking the family car, losing your job, or facing a death in the family.

Some events could be charted as either peaks or valleys, depending on the point of view. A key job promotion, which changed your family life, might be charted as a peak by you and a valley by your mate. Your *is* graph would look something like Figure 1.

Let's make another graph reflecting the differences between what *is* and what *should be* and what *could be*. What *should be* refers to our expectations, or what past history and experience have led us to expect

**Figure 1**

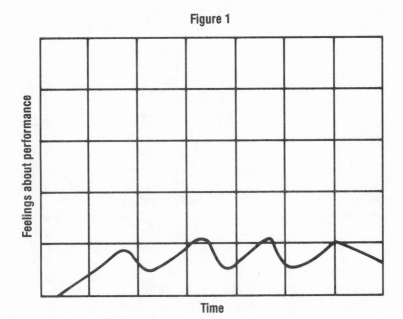

Feelings about performance

Time

will happen. What *could be* refers to what we want to happen or what might conceivably happen—both good and bad. For the sake of simplicity, we'll skip the bad here and use *could be* to signal desire, or the best that could happen.

Plotting your life to reflect your perception of what *should be* happening will yield a higher line on the graph than the *is* line (unless, of course, you think that you've gotten a lot further than your brains and talents allow). Plotting your life to reflect what *could be* happening will generally give you a line higher still. In Figure 2 the spaces between the lines represent the difference between reality and expectation, and between expectation and desire. The gaps in the graph represent room for decision making. Put another way, decisions are bridges to span these gaps.

I know a young man who got a job in Washington as one of half a dozen guards to a certain door to the U.S. Senate chamber. His main responsibility was handling requests from reporters who wanted to interview senators and conveying those messages to lawmakers on the floor. "Joe Smerch of the Los Angeles *Beagle* wants to see you, Senator Mergatroid," he would say. A moment later he would relay the senator's response to the reporter, saying, "He'll be out shortly" or "He's busy now; he says to try him again later."

**Figure 2**

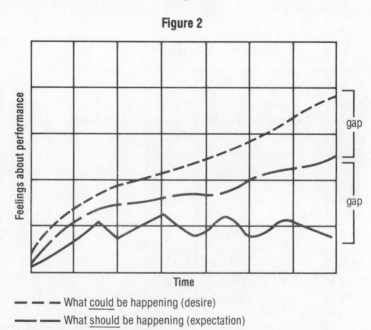

— — — What <u>could</u> be happening (desire)
——  —— What <u>should</u> be happening (expectation)
———— What <u>is</u> happening (reality)

There was nothing particularly distinguished or attractive about this young man, but his family had money and was well connected politically at home. And the man had ambition: he sensed a gap between what he was—a glorified Capitol Hill "go-fer"—and what he thought his connections and experience qualified him to become: a U.S. congressman.

After a couple of years of guarding the door in Washington and keeping his fences mended at home, he saw his chance. The congressman who represented his home district decided to run for the Senate. The young man filed for the vacant House seat. On the strength of family ties, a rigorous campaign, and a claim to have "worked intimately with all the senators," he won his party's primary and—it being a one-party state—the election as well. If his luck holds out, he may someday become a senator. (Of course, if his constituents come to recognize his limitations, he may be out of a job.)

If we were to go back to his go-fer days and plot his graph, it might look like Figure 3. To the young man, the gap between what *is* and what he thought *should be* was obvious. He made a decision to try to close it. Luckily, he succeeded.

Many of us tend to ignore the gap between what *is* and what *should be* and adjust our lives accordingly. On a personal level, we tend to adapt to the pebble in our shoe. We learn to walk with it. Not until we get a blister do we decide to do something about it—to change what *is* happening to what *should be* happening. Only then do we empty out the pebble, replace our foot in the shoe, and walk on.

The gap between what *is* happening (limping from the pebble in our shoe) and what *should be* happening (walking unimpeded) inspires corrective action (removing the pebble). The gap between what *should be* happening (walking unimpeded) and what *could be* happening (preventing future pebbles) inspires creative action—for example, paving the pebbled driveway.

Ted, a business client of mine, was having difficulty with his marriage. He and his wife argued continually about the wife's 16-year-old son by a former marriage. The stepfather saw the son as selfish, disrespectful, and slovenly. The youth took no responsibility for his clothes, his room, or the home. His mother worked all day as a dental hygienist. With both husband and wife working, and the boy unwilling to help out, the place frequently looked untidy and sometimes downright filthy.

One night Ted entered the kitchen to find the garbage bags overflowing. Before going to work that morning, he had asked the boy to empty them. He now exploded. "Laura," he said, "Russell doesn't do a

**Figure 3**

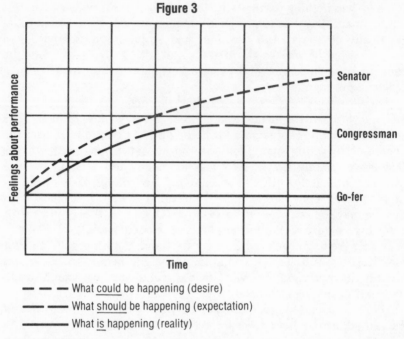

— — — What <u>could</u> be happening (desire)
—— —— What <u>should</u> be happening (expectation)
———— What <u>is</u> happening (reality)

damn thing around here but play that infernal stereo so loud that it splits my eardrums. I'm sick and tired of the mess we live in and his refusal to lift a finger to help out. I've had it. That kid's got to shape up or out he goes. He may be your son, but he's a lazy slob."

Rising to the challenge, Laura launched into a spirited defense of Russell, accusing her husband of wanting a free slave.

And away they went. Voices were raised. Tears were shed. Dishes were broken.

The next step might have been to call the divorce lawyers, but Ted said to himself, "If I am so good at solving problems on the job, why can't I solve them in my home? How would the Seven Building Blocks apply in a case like this?" In his mind he could hear me saying, "Let's smoke out the Issues. Let's ask what *is* happening, what *should be* happening, what *could be* happening." Ted grabbed a notepad and made a list that looked like this:

1. **What *is* happening?**
   Russell never helps out around the house.
   He lets the garbage bags in the kitchen overflow. They can stand around for days; he walks around them but never takes them out.
   Laura and I are fighting about him.

2. **What** *should be* **happening?**
Russell should respond when his mother and I call things to his attention.
He should take out the garbage bags when they are full.
Laura and I should not be at each other's throats about him.
3. **What** *could be* **happening?**
Russell could take on some responsibility without being told.
He could take out the garbage on a regular schedule, whether the bags are full or not.
Russell could be contributing to a loving relationship between Laura and me.

Looking at his thoughts on paper, Ted realized that he was probably making too much of the garbage issue, but damn it the kitchen stank. There was garbage on the floor where it had overflowed its containers. Russell had even walked through it.

Laura was sitting in the chair beside the refrigerator, sobbing.

Ted said, "Look, I know I have been unfair. I guess I have been making too much out of this garbage thing. I'm sorry. But we can't go on like this." He handed her his list. "Please look at this. Do you agree that this is what *is* happening, what *should be* happening, and what *could be* happening?"

Laura wiped her eyes and glanced at the list. "I don't see why Russell should be the one to have full responsibility for the garbage. He's a high school junior now and has lots of homework to do. You are trying to promote him to buck private and yourself to top sergeant."

Just then Russell himself, cradling his transistor radio to his ear, came into the house. "Is dinner ready?" he asked.

"There isn't going to be any dinner," said Ted. "Your mother and I have been having a serious discussion, so serious that it cracked some of the china."

"Was it a one-squad-car discussion?"

"Never mind the comedy. Look at this list. Do you agree with it?"

Russell looked at the list in amazement. He started to speak, stopped, and then blurted out, "Is that what you two guys have been fighting about? I know I walk around the garbage bags when they are full. *I do it on purpose sometimes just to bug you. I have to have my turn at bat once in a while too.*"

"What do you mean?" asked Ted, startled.

"I feel like an intruder in my own mother's house. All I ever get around here is yelled at. So I guess, if that's the way I'm going to be treated, I'll give you something to yell about. I guess not taking out the garbage is my way of protesting that you don't treat me with any respect."

Ted looked annoyed, but Laura took his hand and said softly, "You know, darling, maybe you two are having all this trouble because neither of you shows much respect for the other. You do shout a lot at Russell, even if you are often justified in finding fault. Maybe if you treated him as a responsible person, he'd act more responsibly."

Ted thought for a moment, then turned to face Russell, picking his words carefully. "Well, your Mom may have a point there," he said. "What's say we wipe the slate clean? I'll treat you as a mature person and I want you to tell me if I don't. But if I treat you responsibly, it's only right that you act responsibly. Do we have a deal?"

"Of course you do," said Laura.

"No, let him say it," said Ted.

Russell grinned, straightened up one of the garbage bags, and said, "I could empty the garbage bags whenever I noticed they were nearly full, but I don't think the job should be mine exclusively."

"Agreed," said Ted. "I'd be happy to empty them occasionally too."

Ted and Laura, of course, still have a long way to go to achieve what *could be* happening—arranging their lives so that Russell could contribute to a loving relationship between them. But at least they've made a start. When a problem is masked or undiscovered, it is usually not possible to devise a Solution. By finding out that Russell was using the garbage as a weapon, Ted and Laura were able to work out an immediate remedy, which was the equivalent of removing the pebble from their shoe. They still have to find out how to pave the driveway.

In smoking out the issues ask yourself these three questions:

1.  *Why* **is a decision necessary?** The answer to this quesion tells you whether you have a decision to make. Keep asking *why* until the real Issues have been smoked out. Assuming you are satisfied that a decision is necessary, go on to question 2 or question 3.

2.  **What** *is/is not* **the problem?** This question helps to define the problem as precisely as possible—to separate the mere symptoms from the root cause of your concern. Move to question 3.

3.  **What** *is/should be/could be* **happening?** By focusing on the differences between reality, expectation, and desire, you expose the decision-making gaps.

Let's turn now to the task of constructing a decision-making bridge to close that gap.

# 6

# Building Block No. 2:
# State Your Purpose

The statement of Purpose—what needs to be determined—is the most critical step in the decision-making process. It is also the step most often neglected. Why bother to examine our Purpose when we could spend that time looking for Solutions? Isn't our Purpose self-evident? Don't we already know what we want to determine?

Seat-of-the-pants decisions begin with an unexamined statement of Purpose. Sound decisions require more thoughtful analysis. The typical problem is tunnel vision. We state our Purpose too narrowly and artificially restrict our search for Solutions. The more broadly we can state our Purpose, the wider we can cast our net for Solutions. And the wider the possible Solutions, the more likely we are to find one tailored to our needs.

Unexamined statements of Purpose frequently mask the real problem. If a man is overworked, his instinctive reaction may be to ask his boss for an assistant. He begins to build up an argument to present to his boss, without giving any thought to whether his work methods could be improved or whether some of his work could be delegated to someone else.

In Chapter 5, we learned how to smoke out the Issues. In so doing, we strove to get *down* to fundamentals—and *up* to a broad statement of our concerns. Now we will reflect on those concerns in formulating our Purpose, or (as it's called in business circles) our mission.

What needs to be determined? Why? Let's look back at some cases. Remember Julie, the young woman trying to balance her law school ambitions with the lure of marriage? Stated narrowly, the Purpose of her decision was to choose between her career and her suitor. Stated more broadly—to produce a wider range of options—her purpose was to decide how to plan for a fulfilling life.

Then there was Ted, who was trying to deal with his stepson. Stated narrowly, his Purpose was to determine the best way to get Russell to take out the garbage. But the garbage problem was a symptom of deeper-seated tensions and anxieties. To get down to the real problem, Ted had to make a broader statement of Purpose—namely, to determine the best way to establish trust and respect between himself and Russell (and thereby restore a loving relationship between himself and Laura).

Tradition and habit often prevent us from uncovering our real Purpose, as the senior executives of one pulp and paper company found when they sought my counsel. The company was concerned about improving its long-range planning process, hooking up planning with operations, and using its large cash reserves to make acquisitions.

At my first meeting with the executive committee I asked, "What is the mission of your business?"

The executives proceeded to describe their various pulp and paper businesses.

"But why," I continued, "are you in these operations? What is or what should be the mission that justifies being in these operations?"

After considerable discussion they concluded that "packaging" should be their mission. The distinction changed the orientation of their business from means (pulp and paper) to end use (packaging), from manufacturing to customer needs, at a time when escalating costs had severely limited the opportunities for expansion in pulp and paper.

Whereas before, the company's Purpose might have been "determine the best way to grow in the pulp and paper business," now the Purpose became "determine the best way to grow through packaging." Armed with this new Purpose, the company rewrote its charter and its strategic plan. It widened its search for acquisitions to include opportunities in warehousing and distribution. The Purpose—growth in packaging—permitted the company to explore a new range of Alternatives.

If you have successfully used Building Block No. 1 to determine why a decision is necessary, your answers have furnished a list of clues to help you define your Purpose. The clues are Issues, both logical and emotional, that underlie what you perceive to be a problem. Now is the time to bring your Purpose into focus with a straightforward statement.

Review the Issues and ask yourself, "What am I really trying to decide and why?"

Make sure your Purpose is within your scope. Is it within your power to control or at least influence? There's no point selecting an impossible Purpose. Try to state your Purpose in the form of an opportunity. "Get rid of the pimples on my face" will not produce nearly as many opportunities as "make myself as attractive as possible." Getting rid of the pimples may be only a small part of what it takes to make you as attractive as possible. Many opportunity-oriented statements of Purpose begin with "determine the best way to. . . ."

State your Purpose broadly, not specifically. As we have seen, the more you broaden the statement, the more you widen the range of possible Solutions. Try to avoid statements of the either/or or yes/no variety. Such statements tend to blind you when you scan for possible Solutions. "Determine the best type of job for me" is better than "Should I take the offer from the Phillips Company or the Morris Company?" which, in turn, is better than "Should I take a job with the Morris Company?"

Frequently circumstances force us to choose among statements of Purpose, all of which may offer some risks. That was the situation that my friend Henry faced when his wife, Gloria, invited her father to dinner.

It was a dinner that Henry had been dreading. His father-in-law had been getting his own way for so long that he had become insensitive to the impact of his words—or his whims. President and majority stockholder of a multimillion-dollar plastics company he had built from scratch, R.C. took secret delight in goading his son-in-law, who served as company sales manager.

Henry had joined the company after marrying Gloria over her father's protest. R.C. seemed determined never to forgive his son-in-law for stealing his daughter. It's not that Henry was a dullard. In fact, everyone in the plant had been impressed by Henry's performance—everyone, that is, but R.C. Henry worked long hours, traveled with the salesmen, and had introduced a well-accepted packaging system. Still, his father-in-law treated him like a verbal punching bag.

"Anybody could do what he's doing," R.C. once said within Henry's earshot. "Our line is what does the selling. Hell, I ran this business for ten years before I even knew what a sales manager was."

Now R.C. was coming to dinner, and Henry was determined not to let the evening pass without asserting himself in a way that his father-in-law would not forget. But how? Henry had been exposed to my Seven Building Blocks at a conference of the Society of the Plastics

Industry. "What's my Purpose?" he asked himself. He ran through the following options in his mind:

1. *Determine the best way to tell the old man off.* After asking himself why, he discarded this option on the grounds that though it might make him feel good for a while, it wouldn't solve his problems with R.C. and might upset Gloria.
2. *Determine the best way to get through the evening without letting R.C. insult me.* By asking why, he determined that his problems were bigger than this one evening.
3. *Determine the best way to stand up for myself so R.C. will stop pushing me around.* By asking why, he concluded: "So he will respect me."
4. *Determine the best way to get the old man to respect me.* That was closer to the mark, Henry thought, but it was more than he could accomplish in an evening.

But at least Henry could make a start on earning his father-in-law's respect. It beat sitting still and taking insults. So Henry formulated his statement of Purpose as "determine the best way to start gaining the old man's respect." Why? "Because I need the respect to do my best, at work and at home." Just stating his Purpose made Henry feel better. As he dressed for dinner, he thought of various ways to accomplish his Purpose. He settled on discussing something that had been on his mind at the office for almost a year.

Henry met R.C. at the door and gave him a big, friendly greeting. A few minutes later, as he was mixing the martinis, Henry seized the initiative. "You know, R.C.," he said, "you've always divided the country into territories for the salesmen."

Talking business at home was something R.C. enjoyed. He warmed to the topic. "You bet I do. That's the way to do it and that's the way I've always done it." Once R.C. had taken a position, he stuck to it. To change would be to admit that he was not right in the first place. "If you want good salesmen," R.C. continued, "you have to treat them right. Give them commissions on every order that is shipped into their territory."

"That doesn't give our New York salesmen much incentive to call on the buying offices of the national chains for orders that are shipped to Chicago," said Henry. "Why don't we split the commissions between New York and Chicago?"

"I told our New York salesmen to stay the hell away from the chain buyers. The chains are a bunch of chiselers, always looking for a special price," fumed R.C.

Gloria entered the room. "Are you two talking business?" she asked.

Henry poured her a martini and continued talking to R.C. "I thought," he said, "if I started calling on the chain headquarters myself, I could get business for all our salesmen in all territories."

"I tried that years ago myself. It's a complete waste of time. You won't get any business."

"Then certainly you won't object if I personally draw full commission for all business that I can get from the chains?"

"Of course he won't," said Gloria, joining the conversation as if on cue. "You know R.C. is fair and generous." She smiled impishly and winked at her father. His returning smile seemed a bit forced. But he soon recovered his composure and became increasingly voluble as the evening wore on.

R.C. could have dismissed Henry's proposal out of hand, but he didn't. Maybe it was the couple's hospitality that evening. Gloria had made his favorite dinner—shrimp creole with white rice. Most likely, thought Henry, R.C. had been impressed with his initiative. Whatever the reason, the evening was especially pleasant. R.C. talked about his new boat. He complimented his son-in-law on his selection of after-dinner liqueurs. It was past midnight when he said good night.

Later, as he and Gloria were reflecting on the evening, Henry confessed: "You know, I came very close to starting a big row before I thought through what I wanted to accomplish tonight. This was a lot more satisfying than a big row."

When Henry told me this story, he emphasized that the events of that night were only a beginning. He had deliberately chosen a bite-sized Purpose for one evening: *starting* to gain R.C.'s respect. But recognizing that his Purpose was to determine the best way to win R.C.'s respect was a turning point in his life. He obtained sizable orders from chain stores and earned large commissions over the years. He was so successful in dealing with the chains that he began to supply them with merchandise for their private labels. When he received a job offer from a competing plastics manufacturer, he turned it down. But he made sure R.C. knew about it.

What are the lessons of the story? In stating your Purpose, choose something manageable and positive and express it, if possible, in the form of an opportunity ("start winning his respect") rather than negatively and reactively ("make him stop insulting me"). Avoid either/or or yes/no formulations and state your Purpose broadly rather than specifically.

The latter point was driven home to me several years ago when I owned a small convertible sports car. I had a habit of leaving the top down on hot summer nights. As you might expect, one morning not long after I bought the car I found the interior soaked from an overnight rain. I resolved to always raise the top before turning in for the night.

A few days later, while on vacation in Vermont, I awoke at 6:00 A.M. to the patter of rain on the roof of the motel. I thought of the car, but remembering that I had raised the top I turned over to go back to sleep. Then I remembered something I had not done. Cursing myself, I got up, dressed, filled my arms with motel towels, and sloshed through the heavy rain to the car, which—as I had suddenly realized—was indeed soaked.

Why? Because I had foolishly neglected to shut the windows. In Building Block terms, I had failed to define my true Purpose: "determine the best way to keep my car dry at night." If I had recognized this broad Purpose (by asking, "Why is it important to raise the top?"), I would have seen that more was involved in keeping the car dry than merely raising the top.

A small example, but it illustrates an important point. The wider our statement of Purpose, the wider our search for possible Solutions; and the wider the possible Solutions, the more likely we are to find one that suits our particular needs.

We now know how to smoke out the Issues and how to formulate a statement of Purpose. We know what bothers us and what we want to decide. But how do we look for Solutions? Where do they come from? Our Solutions are a response to the Criteria or objectives we set. It is to the task of setting those Criteria that we now turn.

# 7

# Building Block No. 3:
# Set Your Criteria

When a woman goes into a store to buy a friend a wedding gift, she may or may not know what she's looking for. Even if she doesn't, she has already employed the first two Building Blocks.

Building Block No. 1 asks whether any decision is necessary. She's decided. Yes, it is. You can't go empty-handed to a wedding, after all. Building Block No. 2 asks what your Purpose is. That's obvious: finding the most appropriate gift for the occasion. But what is the most appropriate gift? What should she be looking for? Before she can find the right gift, she has to ask herself what she wants from a gift. To be more precise: What Criteria would a gift have to fulfill to be the most appropriate for her friend's wedding?

Building Block No. 3 gives you the Criteria you need to make sound decisions in any situation. The Criteria lie in the answers to three questions:

1. What do you want to *achieve* by any decision you make?
2. What do you want to *preserve* by any decision you make?
3. What do you want to *avoid* by any decision you make?

The answers to these three *separate* questions become the Criteria by which you subsequently judge possible Solutions.

Here's how the process worked for Maureen, the woman shopping for a wedding gift. She and Renata, the bride-to-be, worked in the accounting department of a Boston bank. Maureen had taken up an office collection and raised $200 for a gift from her and her co-workers. That meant she'd have plenty of money to work with. Maureen's choice was guided by her knowledge that Renata liked to sew, cook, and paint. She was also aware that the couple had rented a tiny apartment and was expecting to move frequently, since the groom was an Army officer.

Maureen's list of gift Criteria looked like this:

## PURPOSE
Determine the most appropriate wedding present for Renata

## CRITERIA
Achieve
   A thoughtful gift, something she'll really love
   Something no one else is likely to give her
   Something I can be reasonably certain she doesn't already have
   Something her husband will derive pleasure from
   Something the couple can enjoy over the years
   Something that will help her sew, cook, or paint

Preserve
   Our friendship
   Her feeling that her co-workers really care about her

Avoid
   Spending more than $200
   Something that takes up a lot of space
   Something that can't easily be moved

With that list of Criteria to guide her, Maureen took less than an hour to settle on Renata's present: a Cuisinart, a food processor to help her make gourmet meals. The bride, by the way, was thrilled with it.

The same techniques—deciding what you want to achieve, preserve, and avoid—can be used in choosing an apartment, a new car, a job, or in making hundreds of decisions that confront you every day. Once you have set your Purpose and established the Criteria any choice must satisfy, you're on your way.

Let's try a short quiz to see how well you understand the Building Blocks. See if you can distinguish the Purpose (Building Block No. 2) from the Criteria (Building Block No. 3) in the following situation.

Valerie was the young manager of a ladies' boutique, the kind of store that specializes in high fashion, high quality, top service—and top prices. Her job was to provide the taste and reassurance that customers needed to feel well dressed. Valerie didn't just sell clothes; she prescribed costumes.

In such a store trust is important. That trust was momentarily
shattered one day when an irate woman burst into the boutique,
brandishing a brown suede jacket. She flung the jacket on the counter
in front of Valerie and declared, her voice shaking with anger, "Look
at this coat you sold me last week." She pointed a big, stubby finger at
a spot on the back. "Will you look at that ink spot? You had some nerve
selling me a coat like that."

Customers turned to stare. Valerie suddenly felt her cheeks flush.
There was indeed an ink mark on the back of the jacket. What should
she do? Valerie had only a moment to decide how to react. She knew
her boss would expect her to handle the situation in a manner that was
financially advantageous to him. She knew she had to calm the woman
down and defuse the situation. She knew she should try to maintain the
trust of the other customers in the store and, if possible, that of the
woman too.

With that background, write down in the proper spaces what you
believe to be Valerie's Purpose in this situation and the Criteria she
should use in pursuing it.

**PURPOSE**

_____

**CRITERIA**

Achieve

_____

_____

_____

Preserve

_____

_____

_____

Avoid

_____

_____

_____

Here is an analysis of the same situation. Let's study it.

**PURPOSE**

Maximize the financial advantage of Valerie's employer (or at least minimize
the financial damage from this incident)

## CRITERIA

Achieve
  Defuse the situation
  Calm the woman down
  Satisfy the customer's complaint

Preserve
  The confidence and trust of other customers in the store
  The confidence and trust of the woman too, if possible

Avoid
  A confrontation with the woman
  Prolonging the embarrassing scene


If you said that Valerie's Purpose was to defuse the situation or calm the woman down, you forgot a crucial lesson from Chapter 6. You must ask, "What needs to be determined and why?" until you come out with a statement of Purpose that in your judgment cannot be reduced further. If you said the Purpose was to defuse the situation, ask yourself why. You'll probably find there's a further answer: to avoid losing other customers. That shows you that defusing the situation is not an end in itself; it is not the Purpose. Similarly, if you ask yourself why it is necessary to avoid losing other customers, you'll find that having customers isn't an end in itself either; it is not the Purpose.

You may well conclude that the end—the bottom line—is optimizing profits without taking any action that might seriously hurt profits in the future. If "optimizing profits" (or "minimizing loss") is the Purpose, everything that happens in the store must be done with this end in mind. The other steps (defusing, avoiding loss of customers, calming the woman down) are merely Criteria to be used in fashioning a Solution to achieve that Purpose.

Let's look at how Valerie actually handled the crisis. She said in a very friendly voice, "It sure is a bad stain. I can assure you we would never have sold you a damaged coat if we had known about it. We can refund your money, replace the coat, order a duplicate in your size if we don't have one in stock, or have the ink removed if that's possible." Then she had another thought.

"You know, I was just about to take a coffeebreak. Why don't we have coffee together and discuss the best thing to do?"

When the woman saw that Valerie was sympathetic and anxious to satisfy her grievance, her anger disappeared. Over coffee and cake they calmly discussed the options available to her. She said she really liked the jacket; she didn't want to wait until a new one could be ordered. And she didn't want a refund, because she would then have to shop for another coat.

As they talked, Valerie mentally added another Criterion to help her achieve her Purpose: to turn this woman into a steady customer. "I know just how you feel," she said. "Let me suggest this. We have an excellent cleaner right here in the shopping mall. I'll personally take the coat over there and see what can be done. If you give me your phone number, I'll call you tomorrow and let you know if the stain came out."

The customer quickly agreed. By the time the coffeebreak ended she had been completely won over. Before leaving the store, she even asked Valerie to show her some sweaters.

Fortunately, the stain came out. Valerie related the good news to the woman and saw to it that the coat was delivered to her home. The woman returned frequently to shop at the boutique. In recounting the story to me, Valerie confessed: "You don't know how close I came to telling the woman she had gotten the ink mark on the jacket herself. But if I'd done that, I would have lost the customer for good. There also would have been more screaming, and other customers might have been driven away. The important thing was to restore calm, and that meant going along with what she wanted."

Valerie, admittedly, was a very unusual saleswoman. Her story illustrates two important points. Often the best Solutions are win/win Solutions—those that benefit both parties. Any of the options that Valerie outlined would have benefited both the store and the woman. Implicitly, her Criteria included achieving a win/win Solution. Moreover, by adding a new Criterion during the coffeebreak—making the woman a steady customer—Valerie turned a problem into an opportunity.

Note that her original Criteria were all reactive: calming the woman, preserving confidence and trust, and so forth. They were aimed at restoring a preexisting condition. *The best Criteria are positive, not reactive.* They seek not only to defuse a crisis but to capitalize on it, to wring advantage from adversity. If nothing else, confrontation breeds intimacy, and in intimacy lie the seeds of opportunity. Valerie established intimacy with the irate shopper and turned her into a steady customer.

To use Building Block No. 3, you must systematically ask yourself, "What am I trying to achieve, preserve, and avoid by whatever I decide to do?" Make your list as comprehensive as possible. Write down all the Criteria that occur to you, rational as well as emotional ones. Don't be concerned if some of your Criteria appear redundant or contradictory. You'll later refine them and weed out the inconsistencies. If you omit an important Criterion, the Solution you eventually choose will be less apt to achieve your Purpose.

Make your Criteria as specific as possible. "Finding an apartment that is conveniently located" is less helpful than "finding an apartment within 20 minutes' travel time from my office." If any of your Criteria are phrased in negative or reactive terms, restate them positively if possible. That way you may be able to turn a problem into an opportunity. Above all, do not confuse your Criteria with your Purpose. The Purpose, as we saw in Chapter 6, is the statement that answers the question "What needs to be determined and why?" Criteria are the measures you use to arrive at a Solution that fulfills the Purpose.

To illustrate the distinction: a man I know insists on demonstrating his negotiating skill whenever he purchases a car, not because he's short of cash but because he wants the satisfaction of making the seller reduce the price. The problem is that he has come to regard getting a good discount as his Purpose rather than as one of several Criteria to use in deciding what car to buy. Consequently, he has acquired a series of tremendous bargains that fail to start on cold mornings!

Let's recap the lessons we've learned so far. We now know how to smoke out the Issues and determine if a decision is necessary (Building Block No. 1). We also know how to state the Purpose of our decision by uncovering what needs to be determined (Building Block No. 2). In this chapter we've learned how to set Criteria that any Solution must satisfy by asking ourselves what we want to achieve, preserve, and avoid (Building Block No. 3). We move now to the last critical step in the sorting-out process: establishing Priorities among our Criteria.

# 8

# Building Block No. 4:
# Establish Your Priorities

In establishing the Criteria our Solutions must seek to satisfy, we listed things to be achieved, preserved, and avoided. These Criteria are like the points of a compass: they help us set our bearings and get us moving in the right direction. To arrive at a given destination, however, we must refine our Criteria. We need more specific directions to get where we want to go.

In most decisions, not all Criteria are equally important. We must sort out those that are essential—the absolute requirements that any Solution must meet—from those that are merely desirable.

Starting with our list of things to be achieved, preserved, and avoided, we must "rough cut" the Criteria, separating them into categories of relative importance (for example, very high, high, medium, and low). Then we must decide which ones are absolute requirements and which are desirable objectives. Finally, we must assign values to the desirable objectives, ranging from some "high" number, perhaps 10, to 1. The Criteria we assign a value of 10 become the standard by which we measure less important objectives. For example, a Criterion we regard as only half as important gets a 5. These numbers become part of the weighting system by which we later evaluate our choices and arrive at the optimal Solution.

Here's how my staff and I used Building Block No. 4 in looking for larger office quarters a few years ago.

## PURPOSE

Determine the best office space to meet our needs

## CRITERIA

Achieve
> Minimum driving time from John's home
> Minimum rental cost
> Two-year lease
> Maximum square footage of usable space
> Occupancy as soon as possible
> Maximum convenience to everyone's homes
> Easy access to Massachusetts Turnpike at normal traffic hours
> Excellent mail service (delivery and pickup)
> Separate conference area
> Better phone service than at present
> Excellent landlord (maintenance and service)
> Prestige address
> Attractive office decor
> Attractive building and site
> Satisfactory parking
> Contemplative view—conducive to thinking
> Flexible use of space
> Comfort control (heating and air conditioning) nights and weekends
> Office privacy
> Proximity to restaurants
> Proximity to public transportation
> Building easy to locate
> Minimum cost (moving and space modifications)

Preserve
> Comfort control (heating and air conditioning)
> Same phone number
> Same city address as now (Waltham, Mass.)

Avoid
> Noise (traffic, building, planes)
> Traffic congestion

Let me point out some things about the Criteria. It's a long list, 28 items in all. Five people contributed to it. Obviously, no office space could satisfy all of us. In addition, some of the Criteria are too general to serve as guides to weighing possible Solutions. What is "minimum driving time from John's home"? What is "minimum rental cost"? Obviously some fine tuning is necessary.

After establishing a list of Criteria, you must separate the absolute requirements from the desirable objectives. To make the distinction, you must ask yourself, "What are the requirements that any decision absolutely has to satisfy in order to be satisfactory?" Any criterion that doesn't meet that test belongs in the desirable category.

With the refinements, our list looked like this:

## PURPOSE
Determine the best office space to meet our needs

## CRITERIA
Absolute Requirements
  No further than 20 minutes from John's home
  Maximum $16,000 lease per year
  Maximum three-year lease
  Minimum 1,850 square feet of usable space
  Occupancy by December 31

Desirable Objectives
  Maximum square footage of usable space
  Minimum average travel time to homes of other employees
  Minimum time to Massachusetts Turnpike
  Minimum rental cost
  Excellent mail service (delivery and pickup)
  Two-year lease
  Same comfort as now
  Quiet (avoid noise)
  Separate conference area
  Same phone number
  Better phone service than at present
  Excellent landlord (maintenance and service)
  Prestige address
  Attractive office decor
  Attractive building and site
  Same city address
  Minimum traffic congestion
  Contemplative view
  Occupancy as soon as possible
  Satisfactory parking
  Flexible use of space
  Comfort control nights and weekends
  Office privacy
  Proximity to restaurant or cafeteria
  Proximity to public transportation
  Building easy to locate
  Minimum cost (moving and space modifications)

In arriving at our absolute requirements, we examined the entire list and asked ourselves, "Which Criteria are so important that no Solution is acceptable unless it meets all of them?" We concluded that we could accept a new office location that, say, didn't provide better phone service than we had at present, but I couldn't accept it if it was more than a 20-minute drive from my home, no matter what other advantages it had. Similarly, we decided we wouldn't rent space costing more than $16,000 a year, we needed a minimum of 1,850 square feet of usable space, and we would have to move by December 31. Any location that didn't meet even one of these requirements was out of the question.

Our next step—and the most difficult task of all—was to rank the desirables. (Obviously there's no need to rank the absolutes, since each is by definition essential.) Ranking the desirables calls for measuring their relative importance. Some will be more important, some less, and some equally important. The first step is to establish the Criterion or Criteria you value at 10, or maximum importance. Then assign values to lesser Criteria that reflect their importance in relation to 10. If you have trouble establishing the values, ask yourself such questions as "Why is this important?" "What would be lost if it weren't a Criterion at all?" "What other Criteria is it less important/more important than?"

When we finished our evaluation, our list looked like this:

## PURPOSE

Determine the best office space to meet our needs

## CRITERIA

Absolute Requirements
No change

Desirable Objectives
10   Minimum average travel time to homes of other employees
10   Attractive office decor
 9   Maximum square footage of usable space
 9   Minimum time to Massachusetts Turnpike
 9   Minimum rental cost
 8   Two-year lease
 8   Same comfort as now
 8   Quiet (avoid noise)
 8   Office privacy
 6   Same phone number
 5   Excellent mail service (3—delivery, 2—pickup)*
 5   Separate conference area
 5   Better phone service
 5   Excellent landlord (maintenance and service)
 5   Minimum cost (moving and space modifications)
 4   Attractive building and site
 4   Same city address

---

*We broke down mail service into its components and judged it more important to have good delivery (3) than good pickup (2).

4   Minimum traffic congestion
4   Contemplative view
4   Favorable address
3   Occupancy as soon as possible
3   Satisfactory parking
2   Flexible use of space
2   Comfort control nights and weekends
1   Proximity to restaurant or cafeteria
1   Proximity to public transportation
1   Building easy to locate

We'll return to this application of our system to locating new office space in subsequent chapters to examine, step by step, how we filter possible Solutions through a net of individually designed Criteria to catch the best one. Keep in mind that there is no right or wrong ranking order. If you had been shopping for office space, you might have drawn up a different list of Criteria. Or, given our list, you might have assigned different values to the items. What is important is that your rankings reflect *your needs* and *your values*.

Don't ignore Criteria that others consider unimportant or even frivolous if those values are important to you. A friend of mine did just that. The president of a small company, he was looking for a site for a new plant. His list of Criteria included easy access to a golf course. He struck the item from the list on the grounds that he shouldn't let his personal preferences influence his judgment. The site he eventually chose was across town from the golf course.

The result? "I spend a helluva lot of time fighting traffic when I want to play a round of golf," he complains. "And I often find myself arranging to meet customers there for a little business and relaxation. The time I lose getting there and back could have been better spent in the office if I'd followed my instinct about wanting to locate near the course."

On the other hand, instinct alone can be a misleading guide for determining absolute requirements. The sales manager for a major photographic supplier insisted that new salesmen bear a physical resemblance to him. It was an instruction easier given than followed. He was 6'6" tall and weighed close to 300 pounds, a bullying, intimidating presence. But the man was so successful in selling his product that, absurd as it may sound, the company's personnel manager dutifully obeyed.

In time, the essential condition—the absolute requirement—of becoming a salesman for the company was to bear a resemblance to the sales manager. Sales ability and experience were considered secondary. Yet year after year company sales followed a rising curve. Then, suddenly, sales began to drop. Profits sagged. The sales manager was fired and so were his nonperforming look-alikes. What had happened?

The company had enjoyed a monopoly position in the marketplace because of certain reproduction techniques it had pioneered and patented. Consumer demand for company products was so strong that dealers had no choice but to stock it. But they secretly resented the sales manager and his bullying tactics. When the patents ran out, dealers expresssed their resentment by turning to other suppliers. If during the life of the patents the company had built a capable salesforce and cultivated dealers instead of intimidating them, sales might have continued to rise, and the sales manager would have kept his job. Instead, he put his faith in an irrelevant Criterion, believing that physical appearance guaranteed sales performance.

The lesson? *Your Criteria must be riveted in reality.* They can reflect your personal preferences, but not at the expense of real absolute requirements. Obviously, a successful salesman must win the confidence and support of his customers.

Some requirements are so obvious that we fail to give them their due. Such an omission can be embarrassing. My sister-in-law's cousin wanted to become a laboratory technician. Her high school guidance counselor told her that a particular university in her state offered excellent training in the field. Armed with his assurance, she applied to the university, was accepted, and paid her tuition.

She had a rude awakening during freshman week the following September. At a reception for new students at the home of the school's president, she waited her turn in the receiving line and shook hands with the host. After an exchange of pleasantries, the president asked her where she was from and why she had chosen the university.

She gave the name of her hometown and casually mentioned that she had come because of the school's excellent reputation for producing lab technicians. A look of disbelief crossed his face. "Oh, no," the man said. "We don't offer courses in that field anymore. We stopped last year."

The poor girl was so upset she almost cried. Since she had already paid her tuition, she stayed for a semester, then transferred to another school—after making sure that the new school indeed offered the training she sought.

Where did she go wrong? In decision-making terms, she didn't give sufficient weight to insuring that her Solution (the first university) met the absolute Criterion (the program of instruction) needed to achieve her Purpose (becoming a laboratory technician).

Always look for the hidden absolute requirement. If you're buying a small television set for your mobile camper, you may consider the size and price important. But if your power source is 12 volts, you won't achieve your Purpose (finding the best television set for your camper) with a 120-volt set, no matter how many added features it boasts.

A small Pennsylvania town learned the lesson the hard way several years ago when it bought a gleaming new fire engine. The first time the engine roared out of the stationhouse, it turned a corner and screeched to an abrupt halt. The engine was too long to negotiate the narrow streets of the old town. In ordering the new engine, officials had ignored a hidden absolute Criterion: that the vehicle be capable of negotiating narrow turns.

Absolute requirements frequently contain numbers. If you're deciding on a vacation trip, don't content yourself with stating "the trip shouldn't cost too much." Put a ceiling on the amount of money you can afford to spend. By quantifying whenever you can, you'll create a more useful yardstick to measure possible Solutions.

In putting numbers on absolute requirements, you may want to play the salami game. If my wife calls me at the office to say we are having company for dinner and asks me to pick up a pound of thinly sliced imported salami, nothing much happens if I eat one slice on the way home. Nothing much happens if I eat two slices on the way home. But if, after it is too late to get anymore, I eat almost half a pound on the way home (as I have), I am going to catch hell.

So somewhere between eating two slices and eating half a pound there is a critical point. It cannot be precisely defined. If I say it is six slices, and you then ask me if I couldn't eat seven slices and still not catch hell, I'd have to agree. Then you ask me about eight, and then nine. Finally I say, "Stop. You are playing the salami game. I granted you six slices from the original pound, but I'm going to draw the line there."

You can use the salami game to help determine the absolute requirements in your decisions, but do not carry it to extremes. Draw the line somewhere, even if the limit cannot be precisely defined. Anything you can achieve, preserve, or avoid above or below your absolute requirement (depending on whether your absolute is a minimum or maximum) becomes a desirable, not absolute, Criterion.

I played the salami game with my friend Ernie in Chapter 4, when he thought that $550 a month was absolutely essential to keeping his aunt in the rest home. But when I prodded him into analyzing the amount that was really necessary, he recognized that $500 was sufficient. So he set two Criteria: $500 as an absolute requirement and anything above that as a desirable objective. If you are working alone, you must do your own prodding and, when appropriate, set up two Criteria: the absolute one and the desirable one.

Don't be concerned if you cannot identify any absolute

requirements. We tend to think all our decisions have some essential element, but sometimes our evaluation is based more on vanity than reality. It is perfectly possible for a decision to have desirable objectives only. Decisions that have no constraints of money, time, space, or other resources are likely to have no absolute requirements.

Only after you have identified your absolute requirements, if any, are you ready to assign relative values to the remaining ones. In this chapter we've been working with a scale of 10, but you can use a scale of 7, 20, or whatever figure will let you measure the relative importance of your Criteria most accurately.

If you are using a 10-high scale, the most important desirable Criterion gets a 10. Anything equally important also gets a 10. (You are trying not to assign different numbers to each Criterion but to establish a ratio of importance among them.) Anything you originally valued in your rough-cut ranking as high, and have not promoted to an absolute requirement, might be valued from 10 to 7; anything as medium, from 6 to 4; anything as low, from 3 to 1. If you assign a 6 to one Criterion, you are saying that it is twice as important as one to which you assign a 3.

Assigning values to Criteria is not easy. This is not simply a numbers game. You may find, as engineers have found, that certain Criteria are contradictory. If top auto management demands both good gas mileage and passenger safety, the auto engineers may have to make a tradeoff. Light weight increases gas mileage, but it can also lessen crash resistance. Should good gas mileage or passenger safety have a higher value? Eventually a reasonable compromise is reached. You too may have to accept reasonable compromises.

As you begin assigning numbers to Criteria, you may have second thoughts. Will you give preference to logic or emotions? Is it more important to choose a mate who has money or one who loves you? Now is the time to consult your values. Some of your Criteria may not be as important as you thought, or you may discover that you have not stated them correctly or completely. Now is the time to restate, refine, and revalue them.

When restating Criteria, be as specific as you can, especially if you are restating an absolute requirement. A businessman setting his goals in life concluded that his Purpose was to "lead a full and enjoyable life." In setting Criteria to achieve it, he originally listed "financial independence as soon as possible, with retirement by age 58" as an absolute requirement. Later he recognized that "financial independence" was too general. So he redefined the Criterion in terms of a minimum income. Still later he decided that "financial independence" was not an absolute requirement, only a highly desirable one.

Another objective—"a closely knit family, with love and respect from children"—was too general and needed more definition, especially since he was setting it as an absolute requirement. He redefined it as "the solicitation by children of parents' opinions," "the desire of children to do things that would make their parents proud," and "communication between parents and children." But what was "communication between parents and children"? He redefined it as "the verbal sharing of experience."

With some difficult decisions, you may want to continue refining, restating, and revaluing your Priorities over a period of days. One woman I know lists Criteria with a marking pen on sheets of paper and tapes them to her refrigerator. This gives her a chance to work on them whenever she is in the kitchen.

Ideally, you should assign values to your Criteria before you have thought of any possible Solutions. If you have a pet Solution in mind, you may stack the deck in its favor by setting high values on the Criteria it meets. That is fine if, like the president and his golf course, your personal preferences are relevant. But if, like the sales manager and his look-alikes, your personal preferences are irrelevant, watch out!

Building Block No. 4 helps in setting Priorities. It separates your absolute requirements from your desirable objectives. It puts first things first and last things last. And it sets the stage for Building Block No. 5: the search for Solutions.

# 9

## Building Block No. 5:
## Search for Solutions

We have learned how to determine our Purpose and how to define the Criteria and Priorities we need in order to reach it. In this chapter we ask ourselves, "How can we meet the Criteria we've set? What are the possible courses of action?" The answers to these questions become our possible Solutions.

If that sounds like common sense, it is. But it is more than that. Very often we consider only two Alternatives: Is she right or am I? Should I keep my present job or take the new one I've been offered? Often too we choose our Alternatives before we've set our Criteria; in this case, we arbitrarily restrict our choices and increase the likelihood of making a bad decision. If, instead, we let our Criteria generate our Alternatives, we give ourselves a wider range of possibilities to choose from. We thus increase the likelihood of finding the Solution that best meets our needs.

The difference in the two methods can be illustrated by a situation that millions of parents face periodically: what to do with the kids on a rainy day when there's no school. We can approach the task from the viewpoint of Alternatives: Should we go to a movie or stay home? Or we can approach it from the viewpoint of Criteria: What are some things that are fun, take less than three hours, and don't cost more than $10? The Criteria method will generate additional options: bowling, a train ride, lunch at a fast-food stand or pizza parlor, a trip to a museum, shopping plaza, or pet store.

74

By letting our Criteria determine our Alternatives, we can look beyond the obvious choices and fashion fresh Solutions, taking the best features of several Alternatives and combining or modifying them to fit our Criteria. That is what I call innovative decision making, and it is the lesson to which we now turn.

We'll begin by dropping in at the regular monthly meeting of a church building committee in a New England town. The setting may be unfamiliar to you, but if you've ever worked with volunteers, you will recognize the scene.

The pastor has just dropped a bomb.

"I was over at the church site yesterday with Bob Wilson, our committee chairman," the pastor said. "The roof and steeple rafters are just about in place. Mr. Vogt, the contractor, says it's customary for the congregation to give the workmen a 'tree party' when construction reaches this stage."

He explained that the term "tree party" comes from an old Scandinavian custom of lashing a pine tree to the top of a structure when it has reached its highest point. "Vogt says the church members usually provide a hot meal and beer for the workmen right on the site. Wilson told him he thought it was a good idea. After all, those men have had to really work to meet their schedule in the face of the bad weather we've been having."

There was a long pause. Then the vice chairman cleared his throat. "What right does Vogt have to tell us to give his employees a party?" he snorted. "They get paid, don't they? If he wants to give them a party, that's his affair."

The treasurer joined on. "Did Wilson actually commit us to a party? No wonder he's not here tonight. He should have consulted us first."

An elder member of the committee snapped, "Don't tell me we're going to serve beer in our church!"

The pastor puffed his pipe before dropping his second bomb. "If we did have a party for the workmen," he said, "the latest we could have it is Saturday of next week. A large number of them are being transferred to another job the following week."

"Why did Vogt wait until now to tell us?" asked the vice chairman, obviously irritated. "That shows no consideration at all."

What had started out as a rather routine meeting had become a hassle. The pastor was asked whether the congregation was actually committed to a party for the workmen and whether a promise to serve beer had been made. "I think we are committed to a party and I am somewhat ashamed we didn't think of it ourselves," said the pastor. "The men have been working very hard to overcome the delays. The sooner we get into the church, the more money we will save in rent on the hall we are using. A party is a fine way to show our appreciation. As for the beer, it was not refused, but neither was it granted."

"If you have a beer party in what is to be our place of worship," said the elder member, "I can think of half a dozen parishioners who will never set foot inside."

"Wilson should not have acted unilaterally," said the treasurer, resurrecting his theme. "He has only one vote on this committee. We should show him he cannot act without us. I'm against any party at all. Besides, a party would just slow down the work. They're scheduled to work every Saturday."

"Look," said the elder member, "I enjoy a drink now and then too, but we don't want to widen the split between the elderly conservatives and the young liberals. Why not hold the party at the Legion Hall?"

Responded the pastor: "If we refuse to serve beer at the church and then take the workmen to another location to drink it, we will appear to be hypocrites. The church is busy enough defending itself against false charges of hypocrisy without providing ammunition for real ones."

"It was inconsiderate of Vogt not to give us more notice," repeated the vice chairman.

So it went, around and around. An hour later nothing had been resolved and tempers were rising.

In terms of our decision-making structure, the committee members were arguing for pet Solutions (no party, a party at the Legion Hall) without having smoked out the Issues (Building Block No. 1), agreed on a statement of Purpose (Building Block No. 2), and established Criteria (Building Block No. 3) and Priorities (Building Block No. 4).

Finally, in exasperation, Helen, the secretary, spoke up. "Look, we could go on all night without getting anywhere." All eyes turned to her. A woman in her early forties, with two children in high school and one just starting college, she had gone back to school to get a master's degree in library science. Quiet, reliable, and accommodating, she had never missed a single meeting of the committee. But other committee members had always taken it for granted that they made the decisions while she recorded them.

"We are tired and getting frustrated," she continued. "Can we agree on what it is we are trying to determine? Is it whether or not to serve beer? Is it whether or not to have a party at the church? Is it whether or not to have any party anywhere?" She stopped to take off her glasses and gather her strength. "Is it whether the chairman controls this committee or this committee controls the chairman? Or is it something larger? Are we concerned with showing some appreciation to the workmen? Are we concerned with celebrating a milestone in a project to which we have devoted years of our lives?"

The members gazed at their secretary with new appreciation. This was a side of her they had not seen. She had just shown them that they had spent over an hour in discussion without knowing what they were trying to determine. They seemed embarrassed, but she continued without noticing. "Do you realize its been almost three years since we started raising funds? If the rafters have finally been raised and the building is 'topped out,' this is an achievement we can all take pride in. I think our Purpose is to determine the best way to celebrate the fact that our church is nearly completed." She picked up some chalk and wrote the Purpose on a blackboard.

Murmers of approval encouraged her to go on. "Now," she said, "what is it we want to achieve, no matter what kind of celebration we decide on?"

"Helen, shouldn't we use the celebration to publicize our parish and attract new members?" said the vice chairman.

"Don't overlook the fact that we want to show our appreciation for the good job the workmen have been doing. That's what got this whole thing started," said the pastor.

Helen scribbled the Criteria on the blackboard. All eyes focused on her. "Is there something we want to preserve?" she asked.

"We certainly want to preserve our good relationship with Vogt," said the elder member. "He's gone out of his way to accommodate us."

Finally Helen asked what had to be avoided. The elder member jumped right in. "We certainly want to avoid offending the older conservative people," he said. "They have made substantial financial contributions."

"Right," said Helen, "and let's turn the coin over. Wouldn't it be nice to attract younger people? We always say we want to involve our youth in our church. Let's do more than just talk about it."

Helen kept scribbling Criteria on the board. The list grew longer. It included minimizing disruption to the building process, avoiding any charges of hypocrisy, and making the affair enjoyable for the workmen. Two absolute requirements were identified: holding the celebration at an appropriate place and holding the celebration within the next two weeks (to meet the time deadline before the workmen moved to a new site).

After the group had rated the Criteria on a 10-high scale, Helen's list looked like this:

## PURPOSE

Determine the best way to celebrate completion of the church.

## TENTATIVE CRITERIA

Absolute Requirements
    Party within two weeks
    Party at an appropriate place

Desirable Objectives
    10   Be consistent with church dignity
    10   Minimize church expenditure
     9   Minimize conflict among church members
     8   Maximize number of members participating
     8   Show appreciation for work done
     7   Make party enjoyable for workmen
     7   Avoid phony actions that appear hypocritical
     6   Minimize chances of intoxicated workmen
     6   Minimize chances of intoxicated church members
     5   Avoid gossip about church serving beer
     4   Minimize disruption to construction schedule

Once the committee had agreed on the Purpose—to determine the best way to celebrate the new church building—it became clear that the party should be held not only for the workmen but for everyone: workers, parishioners, and prospective parishioners, young as well as old. The party could also be a recruiting device for new members.

Ideas began to flow. A local rock group, which included some young parishioners, could be invited to encourage attendance by young people. An advertisement could be placed in the local paper to announce the building's progress and to invite the entire community to share in the celebration. Other churches could be encouraged to participate. The membership committee could compile a list of new families in town and invite them to come.

"That's all very well," said the elder member. "But so far you have ducked the tough questions. What are you going to do about the beer? And where are you going to hold this party?"

"Well," said Helen, "let's look at the Alternatives that have been discussed and see how they stack up against our Criteria. The suggestions so far have been to have no party, to have a party at the church site with beer, to have a party at the site without beer, and to have a party at the Legion Hall with beer."

"There's another possibility," said the treasurer. "We could have a party at a member's home with beer."

"That's true too," she said. Helen drew a matrix and wrote in the

Alternatives. "Let's first see how these Solutions stack up against our absolute requirements," she said.

As she worked, the treasurer thought of something. "Just a minute," he said. "The Legion Hall is being renovated. They started work yesterday. It won't be finished for another month."

Helen noted the information on the board. The committee could not decide if meeting at the Legion Hall or at a member's home would be appropriate, so Helen placed question marks in the blanks. "The workmen would wonder why we weren't having it at the site," explained one member. "They'd figure out it was because of the beer and they'd resent it." When the analysis was finished it looked like Chart B.

"It looks to me," Helen said, "as if we've eliminated Alternatives A and E right off the bat. They don't meet our absolute requirements." The members agreed. "Now let's look at the Alternatives we're left with and see how they stack up against our desirable objectives."

The group discussed how adequately each of the three Alternatives satisfied the Criteria it had established. The result is shown in Chart C.

The elder member was growing impatient. "You can draw all the fancy charts you want to, Helen," he said. "But you haven't solved the beer problem."

"I think we're on our way to solving it," she answered. "What does the chart tell us? Anybody want to try to sum it up?"

"I'll give it a whirl," volunteered the pastor. "As I read the chart, it tells us there are problems with all three Alternatives. Having beer is a source of church conflict and may cause intoxication and gossip. Not having beer will irritate the workmen. Beer is a divisive issue in all three."

"So you are saying that none of the three is good enough because it doesn't resolve the beer question. Does anyone disagree?" Helen asked. No one did. "All right then," she continued. "Let's see if we can

## CHART B    Purpose: Determine the best way to celebrate the new church

| CRITERIA | ALTERNATIVE A | ALTERNATIVE B | ALTERNATIVE C | ALTERNATIVE D | ALTERNATIVE E |
|---|---|---|---|---|---|
| Absolute Requirements | No Celebration | Church Site, No Beer | Church Site, Beer | Member's Home, Beer | Legion Hall, Beer |
| Party within two weeks | No | Yes | Yes | Yes | No |
| Party in an appropriate place | No | Yes | Yes | ? | ? |

V = value    **CHART C**    **Purpose: Determine the best way to celebrate the new church**

| CRITERIA | ALTERNATIVE B<br>Church Site, No Beer | ALTERNATIVE C<br>Church Site, Beer | ALTERNATIVE D<br>Member's Home, Beer |
|---|---|---|---|
| **Absolute Requirements** | | | |
| Party within 2 weeks | Yes | Yes | Yes |
| Party at appropriate place | Yes | Yes | ? |
| **V   Desirable Objectives** | | | |
| 10   Maintain church dignity | Conforms to rigid standards | Doesn't conform to rigid standards | Better than C, not as good as B |
| 10   Minimize church expenditure | Members share cost | Members share cost | Members share cost |
| 9   Minimize conflict among church members | Least source of conflict | Big source of conflict | Less conflict than C, more than B |
| 8   Maximize number of church members | Best attendance by members | Some won't come | Better than C, not as good as B |
| 8   Show appreciation for work done | Shows appreciation | Workers may not feel appreciated if some members boycott | Workers may not feel fully appreciated |
| 7   Make celebration enjoyable for workmen | Workers may be irritated if no beer | Workers will enjoy | Workers may feel uneasy |
| 7   Avoid phony actions that appear hypocritical | Very phony | Not phony | Phony |
| 6   Minimize chances of intoxication | No chance | Possible | Possible |
| 5   Avoid gossip about church beer | No chance | Will be gossip | Less gossip than C |
| 4   Minimize disruption to construction | Workers would return to job immediately | Workers would return to job immediately | Travel delay |

combine elements of the existing Alternatives to design a better one—
one that overcomes the weaknesses we see on the chart.

"How can we *have beer* in a way that *won't be a source of church
conflict* and *won't cause intoxication and gossip?* Or how can we *not
have beer* in a way that *won't irritate the workmen and won't make
them feel uneasy?* Any suggestions?"

"Well," said the treasurer, "we could try somehow to regulate the
supply of beer."

"And what about the people who don't want any beer? Don't we
have to show some concern for their feelings?" asked the elder.

"I have an idea," suggested the vice chairman. "We don't have to
hold a beer party, but we could provide a party with a little beer.
Instead of tapping a keg, we could serve soft drinks on ice. But we
could have on hand a can or two of beer for anyone who wants to enjoy
it with his meal."

"Then you are going to give in to the guzzlers," retorted the elder
member.

"I think," said the secretary, "a distinction can be made between
having a drink with a meal and guzzling."

"Serve beer in the church," said the elder member, "and you are
bound to offend some of our best parishioners."

"Some people might be offended," said the pastor to the elder
member, "if they did not know that beer was going to be served. But if
you can draw up a list of who they might be, I can personally inform
them of our plans. I can remind them that a building is not a place of
worship until it has a roof on it and a dedication has taken place. I can
also remind them that Jesus was not above changing water to wine for
a celebration."

"Don't be hard on them," said the elder member.

"I am in the business of being kind," said the pastor.

"Their feelings are important," said Helen, "but a personal call from
our pastor should show that their feelings are not being ignored."

She added another column to her matrix, and the group compared
the new Alternative F with the existing Alternatives B, C, and D. It
looked like Chart D.

After reviewing the chart, the committee members decided to hold
the celebration at the church site, with one or two cans of beer for each
workman. Having no celebration at all would have defeated their
Purpose. Having the celebration at the church site without beer would
have made the affair less enjoyable for the workmen and would have
run the risk of delaying the work and exposing the church to charges of

V = value

## CHART D   Purpose: Determine the best way to celebrate the new church

| CRITERIA | ALTERNATIVE B<br>Church Site, No Beer | ALTERNATIVE C<br>Church Site, Beer | ALTERNATIVE D<br>Member's Home, Beer | ALTERNATIVE F<br>Church Site, Controlled Beer |
|---|---|---|---|---|
| **Absolute Requirements** | | | | |
| Party within 2 weeks | Yes | Yes | Yes | Yes |
| Party at appropriate place | Yes | Yes | ? | Yes |
| **V Desirable Objectives** | | | | |
| 10 Maintain church dignity | Conforms to rigid standards | Doesn't conform to rigid standards | Better than C, not as good as B | Better than C and D, not as good as B |
| 10 Minimize church expenditure | Members share cost | Members share cost | Members share cost | Members share cost |
| 9 Minimize conflict among church members | Least source of conflict | Big source of conflict | Less conflict than C, more than B | Less conflict than C and D, more than B |
| 8 Maximize number of church members | Best attendance by members | Some won't come | Better than C, not as good as B | Better than C and D, not as good as B |
| 8 Show appreciation for work done | Shows appreciation | Workers may not feel appreciated if some members boycott | Workers may not feel fully appreciated | Shows appreciation |
| 7 Make celebration enjoyable for workmen | Workers may be irritated if no beer | Workers will enjoy | Workers may feel uneasy | Workers will enjoy |
| 7 Avoid phony actions that appear hypocritical | Very phony | Not phony | Phony | Not phony |
| 6 Minimize chances of intoxication | No chance | Possible | Possible | Possible but unlikely |
| 5 Avoid gossip about church beer | No chance | Will be gossip | Less gossip than C | Better than C and D, not as good as B |
| 4 Minimize disruption to construction | Workers would return to job immediately | Workers would return to job immediately | Travel delay | As good as B and C |

hypocrisy. Having the celebration at the Legion Hall or at a member's home would not have met the absolute requirement that the location be appropriate to a church celebration. As the pastor put it, "We should celebrate our church in our church."

Helen, of course, had received training in the use of the Seven Building Blocks. When she told me the story of her committee, she said, "I never saw a better demonstration of your advice not to jump to Solutions before the Criteria have been set. We were playing the game of pros and cons, with the usual traps. We might have been there yet if I had not taken the bull by the horns."

"How did the celebration turn out?" I asked.

"It was excellent," she said. "We had good attendance from both young and old, from conservatives and liberals, and from prospective parishioners. We may have several new members. So far as I know, no one was offended by the presence of beer." She paused before continuing. "There was one disappointment though. The workmen and parishioners did not mingle. We looked at the relationship between workers and parishioners as a problem. We should have seen it as an opportunity too and sought to capitalize on it. We might, for instance, have arranged the seating to mix the two groups."

Let's review the lessons of this chapter. Let your Criteria generate your Alternatives, not vice versa. It was only after Helen had put the committee through the achieve/preserve/avoid exercise that members forgot their pet Solutions and began seeking common ground. Widen your circle of Alternatives by taking each Criterion in turn and asking, "What are the possible ways of fulfilling (achieving, preserving, avoiding) this one? How else can it be done?"

Explore all the options that flow from your Criteria, no matter how unpalatable they may first appear. Don't be concerned if some of them have never been tried before—like having beer at a church site. Don't prejudge them. Let the Criteria judge them.

Seek ways of overcoming the weaknesses and combining the strengths of your possible Solutions to formulate an even better one. The vice chairman mollified the beer and the no-beer forces by just such a Solution: beer under carefully controlled circumstances. Then turn the coin over. Look for ways to turn a problem into an opportunity. In this instance, the committee turned an initial proposal to sponsor a party for the workmen into a churchwide celebration and a way of recruiting new members.

Remember, in most situations you need not be bound by the obvious or stated choices. There are usually other options waiting to be discovered.

# 10

## Building Block No. 6:
## Test the Alternatives

What would you do if you found you had been left $2,000? The first thing some people would do is to pinch themselves to make sure they weren't dreaming. Then, if they hadn't had the benefit of this book, they might draw up a list of things they could do with the money and make a decision according to which Alternative "felt" the best.

With the decision-making skills you've learned thus far, you would be far more analytical in your approach to the question. You'd ask yourself:

*Why is a decision necessary?* (Building Block No. 1)
—Because you'd been left the money.

*What needs to be determined?* (Building Block No. 2)
—The best use of the $2,000 windfall.

*What are the Criteria for making the best decisions?* (Building Block No. 3)
—You'd list what you want to achieve, preserve, and avoid by any Solution.

*What are the Priorities?* (Building Block No. 4)
—You'd list your absolute requirements and desirable objectives.

*How can the Criteria be met?* (Building Block No. 5)
—You'd list the possible Solutions.

But what if, after you've taken those five steps, no Solution emerges as the clear winner? Or what if several parties are involved in the decision and they disagree on the best Solution? Suppose, for example, that the building committee in Chapter 9 had not agreed on a Solution to the church-beer problem. What if someone had demanded *proof* that the Alternative chosen was indeed superior to the others? Clearly, an objective standard is needed to measure or test the Alternatives.

There is such a standard. It's applicable to any decision, however complicated, and however subjective or emotional the stakes. In this chapter we'll outline a numerical standard for rating our Alternatives. We'll learn how to apply it to any problem or opportunity. We'll see how my company applied it to the objective task of choosing office space and how Helen might have applied it in Chapter 9 to the emotional task of resolving the church-beer problem.

Testing the Alternatives involves three steps. First, ask yourself how well each Alternative meets each Criterion. Using a 10-high scale, rate each Alternative the same way you learned to rate each Criterion. *Just as you must have one or more Criteria that rate a 10,* so you must have *one or more Alternatives that rate a 10 against each Criterion.* If no Alternative does a perfect job of satisfying a particular Criterion, the one that comes closest to doing so rates a 10. Second, multiply the rating of each Criterion by the rating of each Alternative. Third, add up the scores of each Alternative and compare the totals.

Here's how one family tested the Alternatives in deciding how to spend $2,000. Tom O'Neill, a shop foreman and hardworking family man, had been left the money by a maiden aunt. He asked his wife, Mary, to help him decide what to do with the money. They spent a few minutes doing what most families would do: discussing the possible uses of the money.

"Let's not spend it," said Mary. "A little nest egg wouldn't hurt when Nan starts at the state university next September. There'll be lots of expenses we didn't plan on."

Tom disagreed. "I've got my mind made up. We decided Nan was going to college before we knew about this $2,000. For once in our lives let's spend some money to have fun without feeling guilty."

"But the house needs painting and the furnace is making funny noises."

"Those are expenses we would have anyway," said Tom. "Why don't we use the money for a nice vacation? Or we could buy a motorcycle and go on trips. A bike would be fun for the kids too. And we've always talked about having a decent stereo set."

At this point daughter Nan entered the discussion. She'd been eavesdropping and had done some scribbling on a pad. "Now, as I understand it, you want to do something we will always remember as fun, and something everyone in the family can enjoy, even little Timmy. Is that right?"

"Yes," said Mary, "but just to keep the idea of painting the house alive, it ought to go for something lasting."

With Nan's help, Tom and Mary settled on two absolute Criteria: they should not exceed the $2,000 limit and should not use the money for ordinary expenses. They also agreed on five other Criteria, which Nan labeled desirable objectives, using the special methods she had learned at a local crisis-intervention center. Each of the three rated these objectives on a 10-high scale; Nan averaged the ratings for each Criterion. When she finished, the list looked like this:

## PURPOSE

Determine the best use of $2,000

## CRITERIA

Absolute Requirements
  Within $2,000 limit
  Not an ordinary expense

Desirable Objectives
  10  Something everyone in the family can enjoy
   8  Something lasting
   6  Something enjoyed frequently
   5  Something stimulating and/or creative
   4  Action preferably within three months (before Christmas)

After studying the Criteria, Tom said, "There are a couple of other ways we could meet the conditions besides the ones we've mentioned. We could get a small sailboat, for instance. Or a console television."

Nan noted the additions, then reviewed the list. "Actually, all these would be under the $2,000 limit, but painting the house doesn't meet our second absolute requirement—that the money shouldn't be used for ordinary expenses. So unless anyone objects, I'll have to cross it off my list. If a Solution doesn't meet an absolute requirement, you don't even bother testing it against the rest of the Criteria."

Mary and Tom exchanged glances. Mary shrugged. Nan crossed it off. The family now had a list of Criteria and Alternatives that looked like Chart E.

## CHART E    Purpose: Determine the best use of $2,000

V = value

| CRITERIA | ALTERNATIVE A Vacation | ALTERNATIVE B Motorcycle | ALTERNATIVE C Stereo | ALTERNATIVE D Painting House | ALTERNATIVE E Sailboat | ALTERNATIVE F Console TV |
|---|---|---|---|---|---|---|
| **Absolute Requirements** | | | | | | |
| Within $2,000 limit | Yes | Yes | Yes | Yes | Yes | Yes |
| Not an ordinary expense | Yes | Yes | Yes | No | Yes | Yes |
| **V**   **Desirable Objectives** | | | | | | |
| 10   Something everyone in the family can enjoy | | | | | | |
| 8   Something lasting | | | | | | |
| 6   Something enjoyed frequently | | | | | | |
| 5   Something stimulating and/or creative | | | | | | |
| 4   Action within three months | | | | | | |

Tom said, "That's very pretty, Nan. But how do we decide what to do?"

"It's really very easy. Now we have to test our Alternatives. Just as we rated each Criterion, so we can rate each Alternative against each Criterion. We can decide numerically what the best Solution is."

Mary looked puzzled.

Nan continued. "We agreed to give 10 points to the Criterion that everyone in the family should enjoy it and 6 points to the Criterion that it should be something to do frequently, right? Now we do the same kind of rating with each of our Alternatives. For example, which of the Alternatives does the best job of meeting the Criterion of 'something everyone can enjoy'?"

They decided that Alternative A, Vacation, did the best job on that Criterion, so they gave it a rating of 10. Since they had given a value of 10 points to "something everyone can enjoy," Alternative A got an overall score of 100 points on that Criterion (value of 10 × rating of 10). Alternative B, Motorcycle, which they rated 8 on the same Criterion, got a score of 80 (value of 10 for "something everyone can enjoy" × rating of 8 for satisfying the Criterion).

They decided that both Alternative C, Stereo, and Alternative F, Console TV, rated a 10 for satisfying the Criterion of "something enjoyed frequently," which carried a value of 6. So both Alternatives earned a score of 60 against that Criterion (value of 6 × rating of 10). Alternative A, Vacation, which did least well on the Criterion of "something enjoyed frequently," was rated 2, for a total score of 12 on that Criterion (value of 6 × rating of 2).

They worked *horizontally* through the chart, asking, "Which Alternative does the best job of satisfying this Criterion? Why? Which does the next best job? Why?" Their object was to fill in all the spaces on the chart and compare the total scores. But as they worked their way through, they found they needed more information about certain Alternatives. Specifically, they needed to know how long sailboats, motorcycles, and stereo systems last and what they cost. Tom promised to research the questions.

The next weekend Tom did some comparison shopping. When he came home, he had a twinkle in his eye. "Get the kids together, Mary," he said. "I have a little surprise."

Mary, Nan, eight-year-old Kate, and six-year-old Timmy were duly assembled. Nan brought out her list and pencil.

"I remembered that a motorcycle has some costs I overlooked," Tom said. "There's gas, insurance, registration, a trailer, and trailer registration. We'd need a trailer to take the cycle somewhere safe where we could ride it. I wouldn't let any of you ride it on the streets around here. So figuring all that expense for, say, ten years, the cost goes over the $2,000 limit."

Since the motorcycle no longer met one of the absolute requirements, Nan crossed it off her list. Mary gave Tom a sympathetic look. Tom ignored it. "While I was at the stereo dealer," he continued, "I found out that an electronic organ lasts 20 to 25 years."

Mary was excited. "Oh, Tom, the fun we could have with an organ."

"Not so fast. Nan, check it out on your scorecard against this other information on sailboats and stereos." He handed her a collection of folders and prices.

Nan studied the folder. "The organ is under $2,000, isn't it? Otherwise you wouldn't have mentioned it. And it certainly isn't an everyday expense. So it meets the two absolutes. Everyone in the family could share in the fun, even Timmy. Twenty-five years is pretty long-lasting. And it's more stimulating and creative than a stereo. A stereo is pretty passive. As for enjoying it frequently, we would get fun out of it winter and summer. It beats the sailboat." She figured a little more and then announced, "The organ is the winner."

Chart F shows how Nan tested the Alternatives. Study the chart closely to make sure you understand how every number is derived. Remember the three-step testing process. First, using the best information you can gather about each Alternative, rate each Alternative against each Criterion. The Alternative that does the best job of satisfying a Criterion rates a 10, even if it doesn't do a perfect job. An Alternative that does only half as well at satisfying that Criterion rates a 5; one-tenth as well a 1, and so on. Second, multiply the *value* of each Criterion by the *rating* you have given to each Alternative. Third, add the totals for each Alternative and compare the results.

Chart G shows how my staff and I tested the Alternatives in looking for office space, using the Criteria set in Chapter 8. If Helen and the church building committee had found it difficult to agree on which Alternative was superior, they could have rated each Alternative against each Criterion. The outcome might have looked like Chart H.

As a rule of thumb, the best tentative Solution is one that scores at least 15 percent higher than the closest Alternative and that also scores well on each of the highly rated desirable objectives. Unless your choice meets both these tests, you probably can't feel confident that it is indeed the best Solution. Before making a final choice among Alternatives, consider how to overcome the apparent winner's shortcomings

V = value
R = rating

**CHART F**    **Purpose:**

| CRITERIA | | ALTERNATIVE A Vacation | | | ALTERNATIVE B Motorcycle | ALTERNATIVE C Stereo | | |
|---|---|---|---|---|---|---|---|---|
| Absolute Requirements | | | | | | | | |
| Within $2,000 limit | | Yes | | | No | Yes | | |
| Not an ordinary expense | | Yes | | | | Yes | | |
| V | Desirable Objectives | | R | V × R | | | R | V × R |
| 10 | Something everyone in the family can enjoy | Very high | 10 | 100 | | High | 8 | 80 |
| 8 | Something lasting | 2 to 3 weeks | 2 | 16 | | 8 years? | 7 | 56 |
| 6 | Something enjoyed frequently | Very low | 2 | 12 | | Very high | 10 | 60 |
| 5 | Something stimulating and/or creative | High | 8 | 40 | | Stimulating, but not creative | 5 | 25 |
| 4 | Action within three months | Very high | 10 | 40 | | Very high | 10 | 40 |
| TOTAL POINTS | | | | 208 | | | | 261 |

or how to combine the characteristics of several Alternatives to create a better, more innovative Solution.

Most of us tend to avoid the difficult and shun the unpleasant. Filling in the matrix forces us to make difficult judgments and keeps us from running away from unpleasant ones. It points out the areas where we need to develop data before we make a decision. It gives proper weight to a Solution that does a fair job on a major Criterion as opposed to one that does an excellent job on a minor Criterion. The process may sound complicated, but it is actually quite simple. It takes more time to describe than to do.

If two or more Solutions are close, ask yourself what your "gut feeling" is. If you have one, why do you have it? You may find it helpful to go back to the "why" game and retrace your steps:

- Did you state your Purpose correctly?
- Are there additional things to be achieved, preserved, or avoided that you failed to state as Criteria?
- Do the values you assigned to the Criteria accurately reflect your Priorities?
- Have you overlooked any other Alternatives that deserve consideration?
- Are you confident of the accuracy and completeness of the data you used to rate your Alternatives, especially the heavily weighted Criteria?

## Determine the best use of $2,000

| ALTERNATIVE D Painting House | ALTERNATIVE E Sailboat | | | ALTERNATIVE F Console TV | | | ALTERNATIVE G Electric Organ | | |
|---|---|---|---|---|---|---|---|---|---|
| Yes | Yes | | | Yes | | | Yes | | |
| No | Yes | | | Yes | | | Yes | | |
| | | R | V × R | | R | V × R | | R | V × R |
| | High | 8 | 80 | High | 8 | 80 | Very high | 10 | 100 |
| | 10 years? | 8 | 64 | 8 years? | 7 | 56 | 15 to 20 years? | 10 | 80 |
| | In winter forget it | 3 | 18 | Very high | 10 | 60 | Very high | 10 | 60 |
| | Moderately | 7 | 35 | Stimulating but not creative | 5 | 25 | Stimulating and creative | 10 | 50 |
| | No benefit until spring | 2 | 8 | Very high | 10 | 40 | Very high | 10 | 40 |
| | | | 205 | | | 261 | THE WINNER | | 330 |

- When you rated each Alternative against the Criteria, did you "fudge" any of the ratings?
- Did you use a 10 rating for the Alternative that best satisfied each Criterion and rank the others in relation to it?
- Did you make any simple errors in arithmetic?
- Can you combine features of two or more Alternatives to develop a superior Solution? In fashioning a superior Solution, look for existing weak points and try to strengthen them.

In this chapter we have seen how to subject our Alternatives to a rigorous standard of comparison. It is an objective standard in the sense that it uses numerical values, which are easily verifiable. In assigning the numbers, however, we are often guided by subjective values as well as by objective facts. The best decisions reflect our knowledge *and* our feelings—and those of the people who will be affected by them. In deciding which office space has the most attractive decor, which church celebration will be acceptable to the most people, and even which use of $2,000 will bring the most satisfaction to a family, we are making subjective judgments.

Decisions can, of course, be made in a vacuum ("The ideal Solution would be . . ."). But they rise or fall on the basis of how well they do in the real world, within the limits of the environment in which they (and we) must operate.

V = value
R = rating

# CHART G    Purpose: Determine the best office space to meet our needs

| CRITERIA | ALTERNATIVE A Another Waltham Location | | | ALTERNATIVE B Wellesley Location | | | ALTERNATIVE C Stay Where We Are | | |
|---|---|---|---|---|---|---|---|---|---|
| **Absolute Requirements** | | | | | | | | | |
| No farther than 20 minutes from John's home | 15 minutes | | | 18 minutes | | | 13 minutes | | |
| Maximum rent of $16,000 per year | $14,059 | | | $14,400 | | | $11,500 | | |
| Maximum 3-year lease | 2-year | | | 3-year | | | 2-year | | |
| Minimum of 1,850 square feet | 1,952 | | | 2,189 | | | 2,020 | | |
| Occupancy by December 31 | Yes | | | Yes | | | Yes | | |

| V | Desirable Objectives | | R | V × R | | R | V × R | | R | V × R |
|---|---|---|---|---|---|---|---|---|---|---|
| 10 | Minimum average time to employee homes | 15 minutes | 8 | 80 | Nearest—10 min. | 10 | 100 | 15 minutes | 8 | 80 |
| 10 | Attractive office decor | Beautiful! | 10 | 100 | Needs some work; good potential | 6 | 60 | Leaves a lot to be desired | 2 | 20 |
| 9 | Maximum usable space | Very good | 9 | 81 | Excellent | 10 | 90 | Not well laid out | 5 | 45 |
| 9 | Minimum time to Mass. Turnpike | Second best | 7 | 63 | Best | 10 | 90 | Worst | 4 | 36 |
| 9 | Minimum cost of lease | Very good | 8 | 72 | Not quite as good as A | 7 | 63 | Best | 10 | 90 |
| 8 | Two-year lease | Yes | 10 | 80 | No | 0 | 0 | Yes | 10 | 80 |
| 8 | Same comfort as now | Yes | 10 | 80 | Not during certain hours | 8 | 64 | Off evenings and weekends | 2 | 16 |
| 8 | Quiet | Very quiet | 10 | 80 | Yes, except for school kids | 6 | 48 | Constant truck traffic | 2 | 16 |
| 8 | Office privacy | Very private | 10 | 80 | Can hear loud conversation in next room | 5 | 40 | Little privacy | 3 | 24 |
| 6 | Same phone number | Yes | 10 | 60 | No | 0 | 0 | Yes | 10 | 60 |

| Wt | Criterion | | | | | | | | | |
|---|---|---|---|---|---|---|---|---|---|---|
| 5 | Excellent mail service (3) Delivery | Not quite as good as now | 8 | 24 | Bad | 3 | 9 | Very good | 10 | 30 |
| | (2) Pickup | The best | 10 | 20 | Half as often as A | 5 | 10 | Almost as good as A | 9 | 18 |
| 5 | Separate conference area | No, but office enough for conferences | 4 | 20 | Yes, if we make some adaptations | 8 | 40 | Yes | 10 | 50 |
| 5 | Better phone service | Yes, but not ideal | 8 | 40 | Absolutely | 10 | 50 | No | 0 | 0 |
| 5 | Excellent maintenance and service | Tenants say yes | 10 | 50 | Tenants say yes | 10 | 50 | Not good | 4 | 20 |
| 5 | Minimum cost for moving and space modifications | Some costs involved | 7 | 35 | Some modification needed | 6 | 30 | As is | 10 | 50 |
| 4 | Attractive building and site | Absolutely | 10 | 40 | Not bad | 7 | 28 | No | 0 | 0 |
| 4 | Same city address | Yes | 10 | 40 | No | 0 | 0 | Yes | 10 | 40 |
| 4 | Minimum traffic congestion | Pretty good | 7 | 28 | Excellent | 10 | 40 | Bad during certain hours | 4 | 16 |
| 4 | Contemplative view | Overlooks lake and hills | 10 | 40 | Overlooks school and ballfield | 6 | 24 | Faces other office buildings | 0 | 0 |
| 4 | Favorable address | So-so | 5 | 20 | Yes, indeed | 10 | 40 | So-so | 5 | 20 |
| 3 | Occupancy as soon as possible | Immediately | 10 | 30 | 30-day wait | 7 | 21 | Already here! | 10 | 30 |
| 3 | Ample parking | Good | 7 | 21 | Oodles of space | 10 | 30 | Sometimes crowded | 5 | 15 |
| 2 | Flexible use of space | Yes | 10 | 20 | Not as good | 8 | 16 | Cramped quarters | 3 | 6 |
| 1 | Proximity to restaurant | First-floor carryout service till 3:00 P.M. | 6 | 6 | Very good cafeteria | 10 | 10 | Nearby diner | 5 | 5 |
| 1 | Building easy to locate | Right off main road | 7 | 7 | Hard to miss | 10 | 10 | Takes some explaining | 4 | 4 |
| | TOTAL POINTS | THE WINNER | | 1,217 | | | 973 | | | 774 |

V = value
R = rating

## CHART H  Purpose: Determine the best way to celebrate the new church

| Criteria | ALTERNATIVE B Church Site, No Beer | | ALTERNATIVE C Church Site, Beer | | ALTERNATIVE D Member's Home, Beer | | ALTERNATIVE F Church Site, Controlled Beer | |
|---|---|---|---|---|---|---|---|---|
| **Absolute Requirements** | | | | | | | | |
| Party within two weeks | Yes | | Yes | | Yes | | Yes | |
| Party at an appropriate place | Yes | | Yes | | ? | | Yes | |
| **V  Desirable Objectives** | R | V × R | R | V × R | R | V × R | R | V × R |
| 10  Maintain church dignity | Conforms to rigid standards | | Doesn't conform to rigid standards | | More dignity than C, less than B | | Less dignity than B, more than C or D | |
| | 10 | 100 | 2 | 20 | 6 | 60 | 8 | 80 |
| 8  Maximize number of church members | Best attendance by members | | Some won't come | | More will come than C, but fewer than B | | More will come than C or D, but fewer than B | |
| | 10 | 80 | 3 | 24 | 5 | 40 | 8 | 64 |
| 7  Make celebration enjoyable for workmen | Workers may be irritated if no beer | | Workers will enjoy | | Workers may feel uneasy | | Workers will enjoy | |
| | 1 | 7 | 10 | 70 | 3 | 21 | 10 | 70 |
| 7  Avoid phony actions that appear hypocritical | Very phony | | Not phony | | Phony | | Not phony | |
| | 0 | 0 | 10 | 70 | 4 | 28 | 10 | 70 |
| 6  Minimize chances of intoxication | No chance | | Possible | | Possible | | Unlikely | |
| | 10 | 60 | 2 | 12 | 6 | 36 | 8 | 48 |
| 5  Avoid gossip about church beer | No chance | | Definite gossip | | Less gossip | | Better than C and D, not as good as B | |
| | 10 | 50 | 1 | 5 | 6 | 30 | 8 | 40 |
| 4  Minimize disruption to construction | Workers would return to job immediately | | Workers would return to job immediately | | Travel delay | | As good as B and C | |
| | 10 | 40 | 10 | 40 | 4 | 16 | 10 | 40 |
| **TOTAL POINTS** | | 337 | | 241 | | 231 | | 412 THE WINNER |

In the next chapter—the final one devoted to the Seven Building Blocks—we will learn how to do "reality testing" of our decisions. We will learn how to anticipate and cope with problems that could confront them, reactions that could weaken them, and changes in the environment that could undermine them.

# 11

# Building Block No. 7:
# Troubleshoot Your Decision

The final Building Block—troubleshooting—is, in some ways, the most critical. It is also the least widely practiced. Its impact goes far beyond decision making. It teaches us to ask about any activity in which we are engaged, "What could go wrong?" It helps us take action to prevent, minimize, or overcome the possible adverse repercussions.

Whether our decision involves a mundane chore (preparing a speech, mailing a package, meeting someone at the airport) or a major one (buying a house, choosing a career, making an investment), careful troubleshooting increases our prospects of success. Troubleshooting is simple to do, but it can be painful. Once we've made a decision, we tend to become emotionally committed to it. The more difficult the decision, the more personally commited we may be and the more threatened we are by arguments that might "shoot it down."

Failure to troubleshoot can hurt in small ways. A student preparing a term paper at the last minute may discover that the library is closed or the resource material he needs is unavailable. His topic may be excellent and his outline superb, but his failure to ask what could go wrong may cost him a good grade in the course.

Failure to troubleshoot can hurt in big ways too. One of my clients invested months of research and millions of advertising dollars in a new food product only to have it fail when the government banned an essential ingredient, saccharin. A company executive later confided to

96

me: "We knew the government had doubts about saccharin, but we had invested so much time and money that we decided to cross our fingers and go ahead. In retrospect, we could have saved ourselves a lot of headaches if we'd made a realistic appraisal of what could go wrong."

There are three basic steps in troubleshooting. First, ask yourself, "What could go wrong with the solution I've chosen?" List all the possible problems you can foresee. Second, make a rough calculation of the *likelihood* of each problem occurring and the *impact* if it does occur (a scale of high, medium, and low is sufficient for most purposes). Third, take preventive action to cope with each potential problem.

Chart I shows a list of problems that a member of my staff troubleshot before presenting a highly critical report to a client

## CHART I    What could go wrong with presentation of report?

| POSSIBLE PROBLEM | LIKELIHOOD | IMPACT | PREVENTIVE ACTION |
|---|---|---|---|
| Projector may not work; transparencies may not project well | Low | High | Arrange to have projector checked out the day before and transparencies run on it |
| I may not project well; my presentation may bore them | Medium | Medium | Use charts and lively examples to buttress points; be animated; ask them questions |
| I may not be able to answer all their questions | Medium | Low | Review data base and master material; clip backup papers to my copy of report |
| They may not be interested in our findings because of staff changes since the investigtion took place | Low | Medium | Concentrate on issues unaffected by changes; make presentation "action oriented" |
| They may be critical of our findings | Medium | High | Stress that findings represent views of interview respondents, not ours. The fact that they are perceived negatively is itself a problem they should be concerned about |
| They may be defensive and seek to justify their actions rather than absorb the information | High | High | Stress that purpose of the meeting is to present findings, not to argue their validity |
| They may detect inconsistencies or errors in the report | Low? | High? | Recheck findings and data base for possible inconsistencies, errors |
| They may be interrupted by phone calls or other business | High | Medium | Stress at outset the 10:00 A.M. break; ask that they not permit other interruptions; let them help set timetable |
| I may miss the plane and not show up in time for presentation | Low | High | Book night-before rather than same-day flight to insure on-time arrival |
| One or more of the executives whose support is essential to success of the report may be unable to attend | Medium | High | Stress to key executives the importance of findings; ask them to let us know if, for any reason, they won't be there so we can reschedule meeting |

company. The report—summarizing the results of extensive interviews with company executives, customers, and suppliers who knew the company well—was to be presented to key executives and managers of the client company. My associate didn't want to be caught off guard.

Positive thinking is often responsible for our failure to troubleshoot the future. We don't want to consider what could go wrong for fear it will upset morale or destroy a consensus. Nobody, after all, loves a whistleblower. At an international conference for corporate chief executives, I conducted a workshop called "The Business Power of Negative Thinking." I had barely begun when one president angrily interrupted me to say he wouldn't tolerate any negative thinking in his company. With head high and face red, he bolted from the room.

His company has since been indicted for making illegal political contributions and fined for violating pollution control laws. Obviously, those actions had not been troubleshot. What other calamities his positive, "damn the direction, full speed ahead" attitude is preparing to unleash on the world, I don't know. Such a man may not be impressed by the fact that the pelicans and abalone that used to abound in Southern California have been decimated. But he should be concerned that his company's stock dropped and dividends shrank because it suddenly had to invest in pollution control equipment.

All the Building Blocks have elements of troubleshooting built into them. As you smoke out the Issues (Building Block No. 1), you may be impelled to action because you foresee an undesirable result from doing nothing. As you state your Purpose (Building Block No. 2), you may be trying to relieve an unpleasant condition that threatens to continue. As you list your Criteria (Building Block No. 3), you may identify trouble to be avoided. As you set your Priorities (Building Block No. 4), you may find yourself more concerned with things to avoid than with things to achieve or preserve. As you search for Solutions (Building Block No. 5) and test the Alternatives (Building Block No. 6), you are seeking a Solution that best suits your future needs.

Why, then, is it necessary to troubleshoot your decision? Because, as you work your way through the Building Blocks, you do not have a particular Solution in mind. You are dealing with analytical tools that could apply to any Solution. Once you've arrived at a decision, you should test it against realistic standards.

Troubleshooting the future helps us to spot problem areas before they are exposed to public view. The action we take as a result of troubleshooting can force us either to correct the problem or to rethink the Solution. Troubleshooting is like calling the AAA before you make a cross-country automobile trip. You can start out and learn about the stretches of torn-up roads as you encounter them. Or, armed with the AAA report, you can bypass them so that you arrive safely at your destination without frustrating delays.

A man I know quite well failed to troubleshoot a family vacation. The results were disastrous. He planned to take his wife and four children on a trip from New England to Disneyworld in Florida. Since the cost for six round-trip plane tickets seemed excessive to him, he decided to rent a motor home. That way, he reasoned, he would save on motel bills as well as plane tickets. When he returned, I asked him how he had enjoyed his vacation.

"Vacation, hell," he said. "It was a nightmare."

"Didn't you enjoy Disneyworld?" I asked.

"The trouble started long before we got to Disneyworld," he said. "In fact, there were times when I thought we would never make it. Our eldest daughter has a habit of picking on the youngsters. With all of us jammed together in that small motor home, there was nothing for her to do but pick on them. Marsha [his wife] had to spend all her time trying to maintain peace. For some reason, the motor home kept trying to run off the road. Marsha was afraid to drive it. Between the yelling and the crying, it is a wonder we didn't crack up.

"When we finally got to Florida, Marsha broke out in terrible sores from the sun. We spent hours running around to allergists and drugstores. We had a terrible time finding places to stay overnight because of the overcrowded campgrounds. Some nights we had to pay just to park in a vacant lot, with no power, water, or sewer connections. The return trip was a terrible grind. Never again. After a trip like that, I need a real vacation."

I sympathized with him. I did not have the heart to point out that he might have avoided much of the trouble if he had done some troubleshooting before starting out. If he had asked himself what could possibly have gone wrong on such a trip, he might have come up with a list like this:

The children will be bored by being confined in a small space for long hours.
The children may behave badly.
A rented mobile home may not perform as expected.
Marsha's sensitive skin may react unfavorably to Florida sunshine.
The long drive will be burdensome.
The campgrounds may be full.

Does such a list mean that the decision to drive to Florida in a motor home was a bad one? Does it mean that the trip should have been canceled?

A famous cartoon shows a father giving his son advice. In the first panel the father says, "With all this talk of war, this is no time to get married. My advice is to sit tight." In the next panel the son is a little older and the father says, "With all this postwar inflation, this is no time to buy a house. My advice is to sit tight." In the third panel the father addresses his middle-aged son, "With this terrible depression, this is no time to change jobs. My advice is to sit tight." In the last panel we see the son's grave. On his tombstone is the inscription "Still sitting tight."

The purpose of troubleshooting a decision is not to come up with a list of reasons for doing nothing. It is to determine what precautions to take to assure the success of a decision. With a list of possible things that could go wrong on his trip, my friend might have devised another list of possible preventive actions:

Bring games along for the children.
Rent a portable TV, if the motor home does not have one.
Make frequent stops so that the children can play outdoors to work off some energy.
Share the driving with Marsha, but let her do the easiest stretches.
Make up for the lost time, if necessary, by doing some driving at night while the children sleep.
Take a nap during the day so that I can drive a few hours at night.
Take the motor home out on a trial drive before renting it.
Stock up on tanning lotion with a sun-blocking agent for Marsha's delicate skin.
Make advance reservations at campgrounds.

If he had done the troubleshooting exercise with Marsha and even with the children, the family might have been brought closer together, with a commitment to making the trip a pleasure for everyone.

As you ask yourself what could possibly go wrong, keep in mind your experience, knowledge, and research, and the law of perversity. The law of perversity says that if you drop a pin on the floor, it is going to roll into a crack between the boards; but if you have made a bet that you can throw a pin into that crack, you will have no chance whatsoever of succeeding, at least on the first try.

At a client conference I asked a group of industrial relations and personnel managers what could possibly go wrong with the plan they intended to present to their superiors. No less than 47 possible pitfalls were suggested. We got them out into the open, discussed them, and made plans to prevent them. Because of our preparations, not one of the pitfalls actually occurred. The superiors, who had been expecting a lackluster presentation, said they were astonished at how well-thought-out the plan was.

Similarly, after listening to the presentation of an advertising program, the general manager of a large automotive parts manufacturer called for caution. "My visceral feeling," he said, "is that it's wrong to associate our prestige cars with taxicabs. Taxicabs have a very poor image. The public has little confidence in them. Do you really think we can impress the public by telling them our parts are used in cabs?"

Yes, said the advertising people.

The general manager, who had been trained in the Building Blocks techniques, then said, "Let's forget my personal feelings for the moment. Take your campaign out and troubleshoot it. Find out everything that could possibly go wrong and see whether you can correct it."

The advertising department went to work. A marketing task force ran public opinion surveys. They showed that the public would indeed be impressed by auto parts that could stand up under the abuse and alleged poor service of taxicab fleets. The task force troubleshot possible difficulties with the Federal Trade Commission, which had been very strict in demanding that national advertisers substantiate their claims. The advertising department doubled the planned test mileage and added Northern cities to the survey so the company could not be accused of rigging the results by testing the parts only in mild climates.

After studying the results, the general manager approved the ad campaign, despite his initial reservations. The campaign turned out to be one of the most successful ever run by the company. Why?

One reason was the product itself. Troubleshooting what could go wrong with the parts (defects, improper installation) and taking steps to prevent the dangers resulted in a parts failure during the taxicab test of a miniscule .1 percent. Another reason was that troubleshooting the initial plan produced the decision to make the tests considerably more rigorous, and thus overcome any possible skepticism about their validity.

If you are troubleshooting a decision that affects other people, you should take into account how they may react and what you can do to insure a favorable reaction. Try to envision a postdecision scene, much as you would envision a home you were designing. Imagine yourself, for example, in the kitchen opening the refrigerator: Will the door open right or left? Is the space designed for the refrigerator handy to the dining area? Then build into your predecision action plan the knowledge you have gained through this exercise.

If you are troubleshooting in a group, you may find your colleagues reluctant to suggest what could go wrong. In this regard, it is helpful to remember the lament, "We never have time to do it right, but we always have time to do it over." One way to encourage candid expression is to suggest that you are holding the decision up to target practice. "Shoot me down" is a phrase I use to encourage critical thinking. If an idea can be shot down, it's better to find out in advance and take corrective action. If it can't be shot down, you can prepare to carry it out with increased confidence.

# Section III

## Applying the Building Blocks in Your Everyday Life

# 12

# "No Time to Think":
# Decision Making Under Pressure

We've faced it hundreds of times: the need to make a decision under time pressure. A customer phones to ask where his overdue goods are. A relative we don't especially like asks to pay a visit. A child recovering from illness asks to go out and play. The boss asks our opinion of an idea that he likes and we don't.

What do we do? We make snap judgments. Sometimes they turn out well, sometimes they don't. But what's the alternative when there's "no time to think"? The alternative is decision making under pressure, using the Seven Building Blocks.

Consider for a moment the seven steps as a series of ocean waves. Our approach so far has been that of a deep-sea diver, plunging in and exploring the depths. But we could also take another approach: riding the crest of the waves, like a surfer rather than a diver. People have used the Building Blocks to make decisions in 90 seconds—decisions in which they have greater confidence than they could ever have had with a snap judgment.

How do you make a good decision when you're racing the clock? That depends on just how much time you have. If you have 15 to 20 minutes and manage your time efficiently, you can usually work through all the Building Blocks. But even if you're up against a deadline—say, with two minutes or less—you can make an effective instant analysis.

The crucial steps in instant analysis are Building Block No. 1 ("Why is a decision necessary"?), Building Block No. 2 ("What needs to be determined"?), and Building Block No. 4 ("Are there any absolute requirements"?). If you go through these steps *even in your head,* you will usually come up with three or more Alternatives (do X, do Y, don't do anything, and so on). You can mentally test them against the absolute requirements, do some troubleshooting, and come up with your decision.

In instant analysis you rarely have the luxury of developing a comprehensive list of desirable objectives and assigning weights to them or searching for *all* the Alternatives (Building Block No. 5). You won't have time to rate them against the Criteria on a numerical scale (Building Block No. 6), and your troubleshooting (Building Block No. 7) may have to be cursory.

I follow two rules when I'm under the gun. First, if there's not enough time and the decision is significant, I try to buy more time. Second, I run through the first four Building Blocks and find Solutions to measure against the key Criteria I have established. Then I skip to No. 7 and troubleshoot the Solution, making improvements where possible. This abbreviated process may not produce the *optimum* decision; but if I've thought through my Criteria and done some basic troubleshooting, I'll usually come up with a better decision than I would have by following my instincts or making a snap judgment.

At a conference I conducted a few years ago for Latin American managers of one corporation, the vice president of operations was startled by a question from one of his staff: "What about the rumor we've been hearing that the company is about to sell Plant X to Señor Gutierrez [a major political figure]?"

All eyes fell on the vice president, who replied, "There's nothing to it." We resumed our work, but no one seemed convinced by his statement.

The vice president had made a snap judgment, without defining his Purpose or his Criteria, and without troubleshooting. As I continued to work with his team, I noticed that he was busy jotting notes on a paper. A minute or two later he looked up and asked if we could take a short break. "I'd like to get some of the managers together in the next room and discuss the rumors about Mr. Gutierrez in more detail," he explained.

When he and his senior managers returned to the room after the break, he asked if he could speak for a few minutes. This time the vice president acknowledged that the company had been considering a sale for some time—though not to the politician named—but had made no decision yet. He also noted the following points:

- He appreciated what had been done to reduce costs and personnel in the plant during the past few years.
- The key economic problems surrounding the plant could not be solved at the local level.
- He was open to suggestions for solving the plant's economic problems.
- If the company sold the plant in the future, employees would be treated not only fairly but generously.
- The company had never walked away from a foreign corporation without meeting all its responsibilities.
- If the plant were sold, an effort would be made to place all personnel in other company operations.
- There was no need for a rumor mill. Regular meetings would be held to keep managers fully informed of company intentions.

After some general discussion and questions, we resumed our work. The tension had been broken. Everybody seemed satisfied by his explanation.

The vice president later told me he felt relieved by his decision to level with the managers. "It was," he said, "almost as if someone had, for the first time, said to them, 'Look, I'm being honest about this, and we have a problem to solve together. The problem isn't one of fighting each other but of finding a Solution. While we look for it, we must continue to realize the company's obligations to its stockholders.'"

He also showed me what he had been busily jotting down on paper to discuss with the managers during the break. It was an outline of his decision-making process:

## PURPOSE

Win the trust and confidence of my team about rumors of a proposed sale

## CRITERIA

Achieve
> An understanding by managers of the current company thinking
> The reasons behind that thinking
> A frank and open discussion of what the company is/is not considering

Preserve
> An understanding that we would welcome a Solution to the plant's problems that would allow us to continue its operation
> The confidence that I will keep managers fully informed of the true status of company thinking
> The confidence that the company will do its utmost to find jobs for them and their people in the event of a sale

Avoid
    Any need for a rumor mill in the future
    Fears that we will leave them and their people high and dry

That was a two-minute decision.

Here's a real instant analysis. See how you would work it out. You hear the screech of brakes. You run to the window and see a man lying on the street. He's been hit by a car. You can see he's hurt. The driver is getting out of the car to help.

Obviously, this is not the time to sit down with a pad and pencil and think through a decision. But as an exercise take 60 seconds and jot down your answers to these three questions. You are about to run to the scene to help:

1. What is your Purpose?
2. What are your Criteria?
3. Are any of them absolute?

Now compare your answers with the instant analysis below.

## PURPOSE

Save the life of the victim

## CRITERIA

Achieve
    Medical help fast
    Victim's comfort meanwhile
    Victim's safety

Preserve
    Victim's body temperature
    Safety of helpers (don't get run over by another car while trying to help)

Avoid
    Victim's loss of blood*
    Victim's further injury*

*Absolute requirements

Note how the Criteria immediately suggest Solutions. To get medical help fast, you would ask the first onlooker you see to call police. To insure the victim's comfort and maintain his body temperature, you would loosen his clothing, get a blanket or some other covering, and reassure the victim (if he is conscious). To insure everyone's safety, you would divert traffic around the victim or have someone else do it. To meet your absolute requirement—avoiding loss of blood and further injury to the victim—you would wrap the wound, apply pressure, and make sure the victim was not moved. And by carefully thinking through your course of action, you would avoid panic.

Even people who are accustomed to systematically making decisions in ordinary situations sometimes panic when the pressure is on. "Don't just stand there, do something!" they are told, and they do something—anything. Sometimes the best advice is to do nothing: "Don't just do something, stand there!" Don't assume a decision is necessary. Instead, ask yourself why. If a decision is necessary, the answer will come to you immediately, as will the Criteria that a Solution must satisfy to be effective.

The daughter of a friend of mine was unable to wear her sneakers to gym class because they were at the shoemaker's being repaired. The irate gym instructor ordered her to stay after school as a punishment, turning away her explanation as an "excuse." The girl said nothing but went straight home after school, rather than following the gym teacher's instructions. She explained the situation to her mother and asked what she should do.

"What are the Alternatives?" asked the mother.

"Well, I suppose I could go after school tomorrow and tell her I forgot and I'm sorry; I could tell her I was angry and I'm sorry; or I could ask you or Dad to write a note explaining the situation and asking that I be excused from staying after."

"What if we were to do nothing and see what happened?" the mother asked.

"You mean it?" the girl exclaimed, astonished that her mother would sanction disobeying a teacher.

"Well, ordinarily I'd say you were wrong in ignoring her order to stay after. Even if the punishment wasn't fair, it's not right to flout it. You could get into serious trouble for it, and next time I want you to do what you're told or you'll be in trouble at home too. But knowing Miss Murphy as I do, my guess is that she realizes she was wrong in dismissing your excuse and would just as soon forget the whole thing. So let's just see what happens."

They did nothing, and the incident was forgotten by all concerned.

If you have several minutes to make a decision, it is often helpful to take a moment and organize your use of the time. During a decision-making conference I conducted for a group of middle managers, I was informed that the vice president of the division would pay us a visit in half an hour. (I had suggested that the executive join us for dinner at night, but he had decided to come at 4:30 P.M. to sit in on the session before dinner.)

We were in the midst of analyzing a situation at the company that had gone awry. It concerned a mistaken judgment in marketing a certain product. The surprise visit made the managers feel exposed and vulnerable, because they had been admitting their own responsibility for the mistake. Some of them perceived the visit as a threat. Others wondered whether the executive was coming to show his support for the conference. Still others suggested he really wanted to sit in the back of the room and evaluate their performance, since "performance appraisal" time was at hand.

Much was at stake, not only for the group but for me, since this was my first conference with this giant corporation. After getting the group's initial reactions, I suggested that we allot 20 minutes to deciding how to use our time when the executive arrived. We programmed our 20 minutes as follows:

| Building Block | Time |
|---|---|
| SMOKE OUT THE ISSUES | 1 minute |
| STATE YOUR PURPOSE | 2 minutes |
| SET YOUR CRITERIA | 3 minutes |
| ESTABLISH YOUR PRIORITIES | 4 minutes |
| SEARCH FOR SOLUTIONS | 3 minutes |
| TEST THE ALTERNATIVES | 5 minutes |
| TROUBLESHOOT YOUR DECISION | 2 minutes |
| Total | 20 minutes |

The group appointed a timekeeper who would give us a 30-second warning before each step's deadline. It also appointed a recorder to chart our decision-making process so we could see the Criteria, their relative values, and the Alternatives, data, and comparative scores.

The 16 members in this group followed the plan and timetable exactly. *With their progress displayed on a chart before them,* they never lost their way. They defined their Purpose as "determine the usefulness of the Building Blocks in solving company problems." After discussing the Criteria, they decided to use the occasion of the executive's visit to try to correct the mistake they had made in marketing the product. As one member explained it, "We are confronted by this situation only because we haven't had a systematic method for making decisions. Let's see if the ExecuTrak process can help us work it out." Two minutes before the vice president entered the room, the group had made its decision and had begun considering how to correct the marketing mistake.

What were the benefits of applying the Building Blocks under time pressure? The group had an efficient method for planning and managing its time. Without such a structured approach, the 20 minutes could have easily been wasted in fruitless speculation about the reasons for the executive's visit. Because this was a group exercise, each member supported the decision that resulted from it. In arriving at the decision, the group became less concerned with *protective* Criteria (such as "avoid looking bad in front of boss") and focused more on *opportunity* Criteria ("demonstrate our new team's decision-making skill").

As a result of our foresight—and our effectiveness in working out the problem that afternoon—the executive scheduled a series of similar decision-making conferences for all 250 managers in his area of responsibility. Ultimately, he and his management committee decided that the Building Block format should be used for all proposals and presentations in the division to ensure a thorough analysis (identification of Issues, evaluation of Alternatives, troubleshooting of recommended Solutions, and so on). From then on, requests for capital expenditures, advertising and dealer incentive programs, and major personnel changes were analyzed carefully before a final decision was made.

Perhaps as a result of adopting this decision-making process, the division transformed a depressed earnings picture into the highest sales and profits in its ten-year history.

Time-pressure analysis can be particularly helpful in emotion-laden situations. At one time or another all of us have said things that we wish we hadn't. Often we say things thoughtlessly and then are surprised when others are offended. Or we say things that we know will make others angry or upset, either because we are angry or upset ourselves or because we believe they "have to be said."

The dress your wife has bought for the office party is inappropriate. The steak is too well done. Her new hairdo is a sight. Or your husband's snoring is unbearable. His table manners embarrass you. The clothes he buys you would have looked better on your grandmother. What do you do? That depends on what you want to do.

Ask yourself, "What is my Purpose?" Is your intention to state your opinion even if you hurt the other person? To make your opinion known without hurting the other person? To hide your real opinion so the other person won't be hurt? Each of these three Purposes calls for a different set of Criteria and, of course, different Solutions. Since your Purpose generates your Criteria and your Criteria generate your Solutions, each step in the chain must be consistent with the others.

Let's take the example of the inappropriate dress for the office party. If your Purpose is *to keep your wife from wearing the dress regardless of her feelings,* you might establish the following Criteria:

Achieve
> Let her know I don't approve of the dress
> Let her know she shouldn't wear it

Preserve
> My position as arbiter of good taste in the household

Avoid
> Having her wear the dress at all costs

With that set of Criteria your Solution might be to say: "I hope you don't intend to wear *that* to the office party. You look like Scarlett O'Hara in it."

If your Purpose is *to let your wife know your real opinion without hurting her,* your Criteria might be:

Achieve
> Let her know I think it's a nice dress
> Let her know I think it's inappropriate for this party

Preserve
> Her faith in her judgment of clothes

Avoid
> Hurting her feelings unnecessarily

With that set of Criteria your Solution might be to say: "That's a lovely dress, honey, but I think the other women will be dressed more conservatively. It's an awfully traditional group, you know."

If your Purpose is *to hide your real opinion to keep from hurting your wife,* your Criteria might be:

Achieve
> Let her know that the dress is fine

Preserve
> Her feeling that she is a good judge of clothes

Avoid
> Doing anything that might hurt her feelings, even if it's the wrong dress

With that set of Criteria, your Solution might be to say: "That dress will be fine. I'm sure you'll get a lot of compliments on it."

The same time-pressure techniques of decision making helped one of my clients react to—and modify—a multimillion-dollar business decision. The client was divisional vice president of a U.S. automaker's subsidiary in a country noted for its sensitivity to American influence. To preserve confidentiality, I'll call the country Proudland; I'll call the client Dave and the line of automobiles the Crimson.

At eight one morning, Dave received a phone call from U.S. headquarters. "I hope you're sitting down, Dave," the caller said, "because I've got some bad news for you. Just before the chairman and the president left on their European trip, they decided to stop production of the Crimson line in Proudland as soon as possible. It was strictly a business decision. We're wiring you the facts and figures that justify the decision. Sorry to have to tell you."

Dave was shocked and dismayed. The Crimson was a major line of automobiles in Proudland. A new model was being readied for production. Commitments had been made for a major advertising campaign. The dealer network had been carefully primed to market the Crimson.

What should he do? Dave immediately assembled his staff, most of whom were already using the Seven Building Blocks in their operations. Quietly and confidently, he explained to his team the information he had just received. He recognized that there would be no value to letting their hostilities simmer beneath the surface, so he asked for some reactions to help them "purge" their angry feelings.

The reactions were highly emotional, as he had expected.

"Why don't the Americans ever take into account conditions in our country?"

"Why don't they ask our opinion before taking drastic action?"

"Okay," Dave said. "I think we have a picture of how we all feel about the decision. Let's see what we should do about it. We know why a decision is necessary. Now what's our Purpose?"

"I guess our Purpose is to do what corporate headquarters wants with the least harmful effects," said one staff member.

"I don't agree," said another. "I think we ought to get corporate headquarters to reverse the decision."

"We've got to decide how to honor our commitments without hurting our dealers and suppliers or our public image," suggested a third.

"It's much bigger than that," said a fourth. "When are we going to get the Americans to stop making decisions without regard for local factors?"

"I think our Purpose is to decide the best thing to do now that a decision has been made," offered another.

While they were talking, Dave was busy writing their suggestions on chart paper. When all the suggestions had been offered, the group studied them and defined its Purpose as "determine the best thing to do about corporate headquarters' decision." They then developed Criteria on the basis of information Dave had received from corporate headquarters about the decision, supplemented by their own knowledge of commitments already made for the Crimson in Proudland.

Their possible Solutions included implementing the decision, seeking to modify it in favor of a gradual phaseout rather than an abrupt production halt, trying to postpone its implementation, and fighting to reverse it.

"As we did our analysis," Dave told me later, "we began to understand that there were good corporate reasons for terminating the Crimson in Proudland. But we also could see that an abrupt termination would have extremely adverse effects on our subsidiary's longer-term profitability, on our workforce, on our service commitments to present owners of Crimsons, on our dealerships, and even on public opinion. It could create a void in the marketplace that competitors would rush in to fill, leaving us out in the cold, perhaps permanently.

"These factors, we felt, had not been weighed sufficiently by U.S. headquarters in making its decision to halt production. We therefore determined that the best Solution was a gradual phaseout of the Crimson. But that wasn't as easy as it sounds. For one thing, we were under severe time pressure. If we were to implement the original decision, we had to begin doing so immediately. If we were to modify it, we had to act fast too, and that would be difficult with the chairman and the president in Europe."

The chairman and the president are household names in the United States. They are not used to having their positions challenged, particularly not late at night by long-distance telephone. But that is precisely what Dave did. "We presented our case to U.S. headquarters, but of course there was no one there who could overrule the chairman and the president. So, marshaling my arguments as cogently as I could, I placed a call to them in Europe, reaching them about midnight, their time.

"They were surprised at the phone call, but after their initial shock they asked penetrating questions, including whether I was willing to lay my job on the line for this recommendation. I gulped and said that I was. I explained step by step why a careful phaseout was the best Solution when all the circumstances were taken into account, and I was able to answer all their questions with specifics they could understand."

Dave and his team later presented their case verbally and in writing to U.S. headquarters, but the die was cast with the phone call. After reviewing the analysis, the senior officers modified the original decision and opted for the kind of phaseout recommended by the subsidiary.

"We developed our strategy and prepared our presentation in a day and a half," said Dave. "I figure we cut down the normal time for making a decision of that magnitude by five days at least. We would never have been able to work as efficiently if our people hadn't been trained in the ExecuTrak process. That single exercise more than anything else made me convert to the Building Block technique."

Incidentally, Dave's strong performance in Proudland—reflected by how he handled this tight time-pressure crisis—earned him three promotions in short order. He is now head of the company's largest division worldwide.

In using the Building Blocks under time pressure, follow these rules:

1. *If you feel the magnitude of the decision warrants it, try to buy more time.* Consider, and stress, the adverse consequences of a decision made too hastily. The ExecuTrak Building Blocks give you a way to logically explain why another half-hour or half-day of analysis should increase the reliability of the decision and how you intend to invest this time.
2. *Once you've got more time, use it.* Organize your time by determining how much you should allocate to each phase of the decision-making process.
3. *Ride the crest of the waves.* When you must make complex decisions in only a few minutes, you may not have time to do any deep-sea diving.
4. *Don't panic; avoid snap judgments.* Question your instincts for reflex action. Take whatever time you have and think through your Solution systematically.

By using the Building Blocks when there's "no time to think," you can keep your head while others are losing theirs.

# 13

## Vanilla or Chocolate: Shortcuts to Everyday Decision Making

There was a time when drugstores and soda parlors carried only two flavors of ice cream: vanilla and chocolate. When you ordered a dish of ice cream, you had to decide between them. Though the options were few, the decision was difficult. You pondered carefully before making up your mind. The introduction of strawberry relieved the pressure. By ordering strawberry, you could escape the awful dilemma of deciding between vanilla and chocolate.

Today we have broken the flavor barrier. We live in the wonderful world of 31 flavors, but even Baskin-Robbins cannot decide whether 31 is the right number of flavors and, if so, which flavors belong on the list. The cop-out is the flavor of the month.

I call repetitive decisions that have little or no consequence vanilla-or-chocolate decisions. We all make them hundreds of times a week:

"Which brand of aspirin should I buy?"

"Should I tell Mom now that Jerry needs an operation?"

"Can we invite Jane and Bill without inviting Betty and Bob, who introduced us to them?"

"Should I take a chance and pass this truck or hope it will turn off up the road?"

"Should I catch the 7:10 commuter train or wait for the 7:35 or the 8:01?"

Vanilla-or-chocolate decisions may be either/or or yes/no decisions. What distinguishes them is that they have few options, are made quickly, and are of no *apparent* lasting significance.

Can the Seven Building Blocks help with such decisions? Is it worth taking the time to apply them? The answer to both questions is yes. The fact is that the process takes very little time. If you learn to apply the Building Blocks on the spur of the moment and in your head, you can quickly resolve complicated questions with the help of a few jotted notes.

The following example demonstrates how one woman used the Building Blocks to make a personal decision. When George came home from work one Friday, he hated to walk into the house. His boss had given him the news that his company had frozen all salaries and wages. He and Sherri had been counting on a raise to relieve some of the financial pressure. They had overextended themselves when they bought the house. As a result, they had been economizing on food and clothing. Sherri had not had a new dress in almost a year. They had an informal understanding that after George received his next raise Sherri could begin updating her wardrobe.

Bracing himself as he opened the door, George prepared to give her the bad news. He found Sherri bubbling with excitement. "Guess what?" she said. "The Burkes have invited us to dinner next Saturday night. There'll be one other couple too, the Frasers. We met them at the church dinner-dance."

It had been at least two months since George and Sherri, in an attempt to widen their circle of friends, had invited several couples to dinner. Sherri had particularly liked Theresa Burke; but as the weeks went by without a return invitation, Sherri had begun to feel that Theresa did not share her enthusiasm. Now that the invitation had been received, Sherri's eyes were shining with excitement.

"That's good news," said George: "I suppose it balances my bad news. There isn't going to be any raise. Profits have been down and a corporate decision has put a freeze on all raises." He felt better for having come right out with it.

Sherri tried to hide her disappointment. "That's not fair," she said. "You deserve the raise."

"You do too," he said. "But it could be worse. There are going to be some layoffs. At least I'm not being laid off."

At dinner George could see that Sherri was depressed. She said almost nothing and picked at her food. He knew that she had wanted to buy a new dress for the Burkes' dinner, and he had wanted her to look and feel her best. "Look, Sherri," he finally said, "this dinner means a lot to you. Why don't you cash in a couple of our savings bonds and get a new outfit?"

Sherri was touched. "Do you really think I should?"

"Yes, I do," he said, mustering as much conviction as he could. "You haven't had a new outfit for ages. That's one occasion when you should feel your best."

Sherri did not need much convincing. The rest of the meal was pleasant, despite George's depression about the wage freeze.

On Monday Sherri went shopping. In the evening, after dinner, she told George she would model her new dress for him. She retreated into the bedroom. After a few suspensful moments, she entered the living room, imitating the sound of trumpet fanfare, and twirled around for his inspection. She was wearing a textured multicolored vest over a long black gown. It made Sherri look elegant.

"You look just smashing," said George, feeling that he had done the right thing in telling Sherri to buy a new outfit for the dinner party. Her eyes sparkled and her spirits soared as she continued to strike modeling poses for him. After a suitable period of appreciation George could no longer contain his curiosity about how much Sherri had paid for the outfit. He edged into the subject slowly.

"Did you have any trouble cashing the bonds?" he asked.

"I thought you would never ask. I didn't cash any."

He looked at her in amazement. "You didn't cash any?"

"No, on the way downtown I asked myself what I was really trying to do: *buy a new dress or be sure of wearing something really appropriate to the Burkes' party.* There is a difference, you know."

"No, I don't see. What's the difference?"

"Well, I could buy a new dress and it wouldn't necessarily be appropriate. Or I could be sure of wearing something appropriate and it wouldn't necessarily be a new dress. What do you think my real Purpose was?"

"Wearing something appropriate, I guess," said George.

"That's right. I wanted something I could feel secure in, something I could wear on many different occasions, something the other couple had not seen before, and something that wouldn't cost too much money. Those were my Criteria."

"Criteria?"

"It's part of a decision-making process I learned at the PTA. We work rather elaborately there with blackboards and relative weights. There are seven steps in all. While I was going downtown I thought about my real Purpose and realized it was only to be sure of wearing something appropriate, not necessarily getting a new dress. As soon as I knew that, all kinds of ideas occurred to me. I thought of all the things in my closet that I could add something to and end up almost as happy as buying a complete new outfit."

George began to look at Sherri suspiciously.

She continued, "Do you remember the navy palazzo pants I bought last year and my moss-green velveteen evening skirt? A smart new tailored blouse would have pepped up either of those. I was thinking of that when I saw this vest. I knew it would go with the pants or the skirt. But then I thought to myself, 'Wouldn't it look terrific with my old black gown!'"

"Is that your old black gown?"

"You never would have noticed if I hadn't told you," laughed Sherri. "The vest was a real saving over the cost of a new dress. I have plenty of things to wear it with. It will give me a variety of new outfits and I didn't have to cash in any bonds."

George stared at his wife. "My, are you clever," he said. "You sure fooled me."

"I know. And I also used my head and saved some money," said Sherri triumphantly.

Sherri had not made any elaborate charts or assigned Priorities and tallied the scores. Nonetheless, she had identified her basic Purpose, established her Criteria, searched for Alternatives, and weighed them to produce a Solution. She did it all in her head on the way downtown.

Vanilla-or-chocolate decisions are no less dependent on logic and feeling than are more complicated decisions. Sherri identified her Purpose through logic, but her feelings were built into her Criteria (she wanted something that she could feel secure in). George sensed Sherri's feelings about the party and was willing to have her cash some savings bonds. In accepting her need, he freed her to discover her own Solution.

When you have a long list of Criteria or Alternatives, it is usually helpful to put your analysis down on paper. Chart J shows how one woman decided what to buy for a friend's shower. The chart took only two minutes to make, but it showed that the only Solution that met all Criteria was a gourmet cookbook. If, while shopping, the woman thought of another Solution, she wouldn't have to hem and haw trying to make up her mind. She could quickly check it against the Criteria.

Reviewing the series of Building Blocks—in your head or in simplified form with checks and crosses—is useful for making all sorts of vanilla-or-chocolate decisions. A Boy Scout troop had to decide on an exhibit for a Scoutorama, a combination exposition and convention.

**CHART J    Purpose: Determine the most appropriate present
for Linda's engagement**

| CRITERIA | ALTERNATIVE A Set of Crystal | ALTERNATIVE B Wooden Bowl | ALTERNATIVE C Towels | ALTERNATIVE D Bedding | ALTERNATIVE E Gourmet Cookbook |
|---|---|---|---|---|---|
| Practical | ✔ | ✔ | ✔ | ✔ | ✔ |
| Attractive | ✔ | ✔ | ✔ | ✔ | ✔ |
| Unusual (avoid duplicate gifts) | ? | X | X | X | ✔ |
| Memorable | ✔ | ✔ | ✔ | ✔ | ✔ |
| Something both she and her fiance would enjoy | X | X | X | X | ✔ |
| $25 to $50 | ✔ | ✔ | ✔ | ✔ | ✔ |

The decision was hardly a momentous one; no one's life would be changed by the outcome. Nonetheless, the scoutmaster (a friend of mine) chose to use the Building Blocks to help the boys come to a decision.

Developing a statement of Purpose was easy. The boys quickly decided that their Purpose was to "determine what our exhibit at the Scoutorama should be." Having established that Purpose, they immediately began searching for Solutions, without first establishing Criteria. The scoutmaster let them wander for a few minutes and then suggested that they could reach a decision more easily if they knew what they were trying to accomplish. Their adolescent minds promptly produced the following list:

Encourage visitor involvement
Be something we are expert in
Have a scouting theme
Be original
Be fun for everyone (us and visitors)

The scoutmaster then asked the boys to suggest Solutions. They produced about 20 possibilities but began arguing about which ones were better. "Boys are no different from businesspeople," observed my friend. "They began to weigh the relative merits without regard for their Criteria, and the debate was dominated by the more aggressive members. To get them back on the track, I asked the patrol leader to list all the possibilities on the blackboard. With the help of the scouts, he then rated them against the Criteria.

"Of the 20 possible activities, we chose the six with the highest scores: Indian lore, realistic first-aid, fire-building techniques, slide show of a wilderness trip, building a tall flagpole, and cooking donuts. The boys divided into six groups, one for each project, and went to work. We had one of the best exhibits at the Scoutorama, not only because of the subjects but because the boys were committed to the project. The decisions were made by the group, not by me or the more aggressive types. More important, the boys had learned a valuable lesson in decision making."

Sometimes an apparently routine vanilla-or-chocolate decision can mask a really important problem. We go through life making the same monotonous choices *without being aware that we often have other choices*. No one tells us that strawberry is also on the menu or that if we look hard enough we may find a creme-de-menthe parfait.

To take an extreme example: once, as part of an exercise at a business seminar, I asked the participants to think of a routine decision they made every day that they had resentful or conflicting feelings about. One engineer suddenly asked himself, "Why do I have to take the 7:10 train every morning? What would be wrong with taking the 7:35? In fact, now that I think of it, why take any train at all? Could I move closer to work or change my job?"

Examining a vanilla-or-chocolate decision eventually led this man to seek broader horizons. He not only changed his job but changed his career. (The decision, of course, was not reached without careful analysis and discussion with his family.) We'll examine how the Seven Building Blocks can be applied in job and career decisions in a later chapter.

Working a simple vanilla-or-chocolate issue with a friend, relative, or business associate increases understanding and communication; it produces better, more confident decisions. The process will not take time. It will *save* time and avoid frustration. If you share the decision with those who have to live with the results, you will gain a measure of built-in support that can spell the difference between success and failure.

# 14

## Stretching Your Paycheck:
## The Building Blocks and
## Family Financing

If you are a millionaire, you probably have no family budget problems. Most of us, however, are engaged in a constant struggle to stretch our paychecks to cover all the things we need and want.

There are two common methods of coping with the problem. One is to avoid it altogether and hope that everything will come out all right. A woman I know looks upon budgets with the horror she reserves for door-to-door Bible salesmen. "Don't tell me to be logical and businesslike," she says. "Life is too short. I have enough things to worry about without spending time on a budget."

The other method involves detailed planning, keeping records in little envelopes with different labels for rent, food, recreation, savings, and so on. How much should go into each envelope? Buy one of the many books on the subject and you'll learn the correct percentages for your particular income and expenses. The trouble with this method is that, if you're like most people, your budget needs are constantly changing. There is no way you can set up a system, dust your hands off, and say, "Well, that's that."

Instead, you're going to be faced with an unending series of budget decisions. What you need is not an ironclad budget but a *method of making budget decisions* that will suit your needs at any particular time. If you think I'm going to recommend the Seven Building Blocks, you're right.

If you don't make budget decisions for yourself, someone else will. Your insurance agent, who earns a commission on every premium you pay for the rest of your life, would love to dissect your paycheck for you. The manufacturers of nationally advertised goodies, who design products with built-in obsolescence, would be glad to make your budget decisions. Your friendly finance company, which charges 18½ percent annual interest, would be delighted to give you advice on how to organize your finances. And Uncle Sam limits your room for decision by taking his cut off the top, through social security and payroll taxes.

With today's high interest rates on loans, it is more important than ever to make your own budget decisions. How can the Seven Building Blocks help you to budget? In two ways.

The first way is in drawing up a budget. Begin by defining your Purpose, which will probably be a variation of "determine the best way to divide up the family income this month (or this week)." Then identify the expenses that have to be met (mortgage payment or rent, loan repayment, and so on). These fixed expenses, which have to be met *no matter what*, are your absolute requirements. Other expenses, often called variable or discretionary expenses, become your desirable objectives. Assign Priorities to them on a month-to-month basis to determine what to pay, what to postpone paying, and what new expenditures to consider. The family budgeting checklist in Appendix B will assist you in drawing up your budget.

The second way the Building Blocks help is in making purchasing decisions. Here you can involve the entire family if you wish. As you work together to smoke out the Issues, state your Purpose, set your Criteria, and test the Alternatives, you may find that emotional problems become more manageable and the range of choices broader.

Ben Nathanson, a technical serviceman for a large electronics company, had more than his share of emotion-laden budget problems. A wiry man of high intelligence and equally high blood pressure, he was driving hard for advancement within his company. Settling into his airplane seat and methodically fastening his seatbelt, he began to review the events of the past 24 hours.

He had come home with the news that he had to catch the morning flight to Chicago to straighten out a production problem for one of the company's largest customers. Barbara, his wife, greeted his news with an announcement of her own. The washing machine had broken down, spilling water and oil all over the kitchen floor.

"I told you we should have gotten a new machine," she said. "Now you're going to run off to Chicago and leave me with this mess."

"Did you call the repairman?" he asked.

"Yes, and he told me that if it was anything major it could run close to $100. I don't think we should throw good money after bad."

As he accepted a cup of coffee from the stewardess, Ben thought how lucky he had been to fix the washing machine himself. He'd always been handy with machinery and tools. It was one way of stretching the budget, and he always felt good when he made a repair that would stump the average homeowner. He had had to stay up late to put a new seal in the transmission. He was elated when he ran a perfect test cycle, but somehow his wife had seemed almost unhappy with his success. What was the matter? A new washing machine would have put a severe crimp on Christmas. They had already agreed that the kids' orthodonture bills would mean no big Christmas presents.

When his plane landed in Chicago, Ben was met at the airport by the company's local salesman. As they drove to the customer's plant, he tried to put his mind on the customer's problems but kept coming back to his own. "Why am I in such a budget bind?" he thought. "If my father had made as much money as I do, he would have considered himself wealthy. Sure there is inflation, but somehow I've let things get out of control. Barbara and I are constantly fighting about money."

At the customer's plant it became clear that Ben would have to stay over for a second day. When the salesman dropped him off at a motel, he phoned his wife.

"Ben," she said, "the washing machine broke down again. It lasted for only one wash. There's oil and water all over the floor again." Oddly enough, she sounded happy.

"I'll fix it again when I get home," said Ben.

"Oh, no you won't. I'm going to order a new machine," said Barbara. "I can get delivery in a few days. Our credit card will cover it."

Ben could feel his blood pressure rising. "And who do you think is going to cover the credit card? Santa Claus? Look, Barbara, you know money is tight right now. We're still paying for the waterproofing job we needed after that big storm last fall flooded the basement."

"Well, what am I supposed to do with the dirty clothes, eat them?"

"I could try fixing it again when I get home."

"Look, Ben, how many times have you tried that already? Let's face it, it's no use. As I see it, we have two choices: either we buy a new machine or we get a serviceman to repair the old one. You know what my choice is."

"I know, sweetheart," Ben answered. "But let's see if we can think this through. What would a repairman charge?"

"Well, I already had him out. With you gone, I panicked when the thing broke down again. He says we need a new transmission. It would be $80, but he charged me $15 for the service call and he'd apply the cost of the call toward the total bill if we went ahead, so it would only be $65. But we'd be taking a chance, because you never know when something else will go wrong."

"Let's stop and analyze this situation for a minute," said Ben, remembering a seminar on the Seven Building Blocks he had attended at work a month before. "We both agree a decision is necessary because the dirty clothes have to be washed. It seems to me what we are trying to determine is *the best way to get the clothes washed,* not *whether we should fix the old machine or get a new one.* What do you think?"

"What's the difference?" snapped Barbara, betraying impatience with her husband's line of questions.

"The difference is that there may be other ways to get the clothes washed than those two choices. Like maybe buying a used washing machine until the Christmas bills are behind us or using the laundromat."

There was dead silence on the line. Finally Barbara said, "Just what is this 'we' business, Ben? Are you pregnant? It's not 'we,' it's me. You're asking me to traipse back and forth to the laundromat with the kids? No thanks. I don't need that aggravation. Besides, I don't have the time."

"Okay," said Ben. "Then whatever we do, we want to save your time. That's an important Criterion. Minimizing cost is important too. Anything else?"

"What kind of game are you playing anyway?" asked Barbara.

Ben outlined the Building Block process to her, then returned to the subject of setting Criteria.

"Well," said Barbara, "I want to settle this thing once and for all and be ready to operate again by the weekend, Saturday at the latest. And I want a machine at least as large as the one we have now, which holds 14 pounds." Then she added, "I'm beginning to get the idea. Just how important is it that you fix the machine yourself in order to build up your ego?"

It was a fair question, thought Ben. He swallowed and then said, "It's not very important at all. In fact, it doesn't even belong on the list of things to achieve." It felt good to say it. After a moment he decided there was something else that could stand saying. "How important is it that I buy a new washing machine in order to prove I care about you?"

There was silence on the line. Finally Barbara said, "Don't worry about it. You can prove it some other way."

"Are you available for dinner out Saturday night?"

"Not unless we get this thing settled!"

They agreed on four possible Solutions: buying a new machine, buying a used one, calling in the repairman, and (despite Barbara's misgivings) letting Ben fix it himself. The laundromat did not meet the absolute Criterion of saving Barbara's time.

"Tell you what," he said, "you work on choosing the best Solution. When I get back tomorrow night, show me what you've come up with and we'll make a decision."

When Ben hung up, he thought, "Well, at least we didn't have a fight. If getting a new washing machine turns out to be the best Solution, so be it. At least I'll know why. And Barbara will know that we have to make the money up elsewhere."

It was late the next night before Ben could get a return flight. When he drove into his driveway the children were asleep. Barbara was waiting for him.

"Are you hungry?" she asked. "Shall I cook a frozen pizza? There's beer in the refrigerator."

Ben became suspicious.

"I've done some thinking," said Barbara. "About the washing machine, using your Building Blocks."

"Here it comes," he thought. Aloud he said, "And what have you decided?"

"Well," she said, handing him a sheet of paper, "check my figuring, but I think buying a new transmission comes out 20 percent better than anything else. I was worried about reliability, but I checked with the repairman. He said a replacement transmission comes with a year's guarantee, the same as a new machine or a used machine."

"How do we know something else won't go wrong with the old machine?" asked Ben.

"We don't know for sure," replied Barbara. "But when the repairman checked it over, he said he thought everything else was in good shape. We'd be taking a chance, but if we got even another year out of this machine it would be worth it. The repairman says it should last at least that long."

"What about the Alternative of getting a new machine? How does that do?"

"It would be more than twice as expensive as having the old one fixed, and we would have to spend a couple of evenings shopping."

"What about getting a used machine?"

"It would be a gamble we just can't afford. And it might take a while to find one with a 14-pound capacity."

Ben moistened his lips and decided to push ahead. "Suppose I fix it myself?"

"It would take you all day Saturday, and saving your time is one of my Criteria. Any man who's been away all week is entitled to a day of rest. Besides, you promised me dinner out Saturday night."

The family got the machine repaired. It lasted 11 months, but by that time Ben had gotten a raise and was able to buy a new machine. He considered the $65 repair money well spent, particularly after Barbara pointed out that it worked out to only $6 a month.

Barbara's analysis is shown in Chart K.

As a general rule, family arguments over money stem from disagreements over Solutions—over the ways money should be spent or has been spent. Rare is the family that has not been heard arguing along these lines: "You had no business buying X when you know we need Y" or "How can you even think of buying Z when . . . ?"

The Seven Building Blocks will not eliminate all money arguments. But if you use them correctly, you will find your arguments fewer and less emotional. The reason? The Building Blocks take the attention that is usually focused on debating the pros and cons of Solutions and redirect it to establishing Criteria and Priorities, which rarely generate as much controversy.

Moreover, because the search for Criteria—and subsequently Alternatives—is designed to be as comprehensive as possible, all suggestions are welcome, not merely those that serve preconceived ends. The decision-making process thus becomes a *collaborative* effort, rather than an *adversary* process in which one party seeks to impose his or her will on another. If all family members participate, the process can be as much a way of drawing the family together as is the desired Solution.

That's exactly how it worked for a family I know quite well. The father, a middle-aged businessman, had always said no to his family's request for an outdoor swimming pool. Basically, Hank thought backyard pools were an extravagance. He did not want one for his family. Ocassionally, if someone pressed him on the issue, Hank would lose his temper.

One argument about the pool became so heated that it cast a gloom over the household for days. It was weeks before anyone could summon up the courage to raise the subject again. This time it was Hank's 16-year-old son, Larry, who had carefully worked out his strategy in

**CHART K    Purpose: Determine the best way to get clothes washed**

V = value
R = rating

| | CRITERIA | ALTERNATIVE A — Have Ben Repair | | | ALTERNATIVE B — Have Serviceman Repair | | | ALTERNATIVE C — Buy New Washer | | | ALTERNATIVE D — Buy Used Washer with One-Year Guarantee | | | ALTERNATIVE E — Use Laundromat |
|---|---|---|---|---|---|---|---|---|---|---|---|---|---|---|
| | | | R | V × R | | R | V × R | | R | V × R | | R | V × R | |
| | **Absolute Requirement** | | | | | | | | | | | | | |
| | 14-pound capacity | Yes | | | Yes | | | Yes | | | Yes | | | Yes |
| | No loss of Barbara's time once decision is carried out | Yes | | | Yes | | | Yes | | | Yes | | | No |
| **V** | **Desirable Objectives** | | | | | | | | | | | | | |
| 10 | Machine to last as long as possible | One year | 3 | 30 | Probably 2 to 4 years, if lucky | 7 | 70 | Best; up to 10 years | 10 | 100 | Second best; up to 5 years | 8 | 80 | |
| 10 | Minimum cost | Best; $30 or so for parts | 10 | 100 | Second best; $65 more | 7 | 70 | Worst; $250 to $300 | 0 | 0 | Second worst; $100 to $125 | 4 | 40 | |
| 8 | Minimum mental anguish | Worst | 2 | 16 | Second best | 6 | 48 | Best | 10 | 80 | Worse than B because of bigger investment | 5 | 40 | |
| 8 | Action by Saturday | Yes | 10 | 80 | Yes | 10 | 80 | May have to wait for delivery | 6 | 48 | May have to wait for delivery | 6 | 48 | |
| 5 | Minimum loss of Ben and Barbara's time (fixing or shopping) | 8 hours to fix up? | 2 | 10 | No time loss | 10 | 50 | 2 evenings shopping | 7 | 35 | 2 or more evenings shopping | 5 | 25 | |
| | **TOTAL POINTS** | | | 236 | THE WINNER | | 318 | | | 263 | | | 233 | |

advance. Larry waited until a quiet Saturday afternoon during halftime of a football game his father was watching on television. It was a stroke of luck, he thought, that the team Hank favored was ahead.

"Dad," Larry began, "I know you don't like the idea of a swimming pool, but it occurred to me that since the rest of us do, the best way to resolve it is by using the Building Blocks you're always talking about to help make decisions."

Hank smiled as if to say, "Boy, you have to give that kid credit."

Larry took the smile as a sign of approval and continued his well-rehearsed speech. "What if the whole family reserved some time and applied the Building Blocks to the question of a swimming pool? Would you be willing to abide by the results?"

Hank started to laugh. "How can I refuse a request like that? Okay, son, after dinner tonight let's play Building Blocks."

Larry, feeling triumphant, informed his mother, Marge, and 13-year-old brother, Donny, that Dad had snapped at the bait. "The showdown's tonight," he added, punching the air as if vanquishing a foe.

After the dishes were done that evening, the family gathered for the discussion. Hank had developed his own strategy for the session. He acted immediately to seize the initiative and demonstrate his superior knowledge of the Building Blocks. "If we're going to do this thing right, we have to begin at the beginning. First of all, why do we have to do anything? Why is a decision necessary?"

Marge was ready with the answer. "Because you said the other day that the business is doing very well and you're thinking of investing $10,000, but you're not sure what to invest it in."

The boys nodded in agreement.

Hank looked startled. "Marge, I thought I told you that in confidence. Did you go and tell the kids?"

Now it was Marge's turn to be startled. "Why, Hank, you said that yourself at the dinner table last week. Everyone heard you. Don't you remember?"

Hank remembered and nodded reluctantly. "I guess I did, that's true. But we're not going to prejudice our decision by limiting our search to a swimming pool. What's the real Purpose of our decision? What needs to be determined?"

"How to get you to agree to a swimming pool," said Donny innocently.

His mother cut him off. "No, son. That may be what the three of us feel we want, but we have no way of knowing if it's the best Solution, because we haven't considered any others." She added, "I think our Purpose is to determine the best way to invest $10,000."

"Hey, that's good, Mom," said Larry.

Hank agreed. They proceeded to list the things they wanted to achieve, preserve, and avoid by any Solution they chose and ended up with this list:

## PURPOSE
Determine the best way to invest $10,000

## CRITERIA

Absolute Requirements
   No more than $10,000
   Action by next summer (six months from now)

Desirable Objectives
   10   Something the entire family can enjoy
    9   Something to draw the family together
    8   Something we won't outgrow as kids get older
    7   Something to enjoy as much of the year as possible
    7   Something to help Dad relax
    7   Minimum cost
    4   Something to do with friends
    3   Something that adds value to house (for eventual resale)

After studying the list, the family came up with these Alternatives:

## POSSIBLE SOLUTIONS

   Swimming pool
   House game-room addition with ping-pong and pool table
   Vacation, either in Europe or in California and Grand Canyon
   Less expensive vacation, plus smaller game-room addition
   Join a swim club, plus game-room addition
   Join a swim club, plus vacation
   Rent a cottage at the beach, plus game-room addition
   Rent a cottage at the beach, plus vacation

Hank and Larry were elected a committee of two to research costs of the various Alternatives. They got estimates from two contractors on the addition and the pool. Marge's brother-in-law, a travel agent, gave them prices for package and do-it-yourself vacations. They made long-distance phone calls to check with a realtor on beach cottage rates.

At a family conference two weeks later they cranked the price information into their Alternatives; then each member rated the Alternatives against the Criteria. The pool won hands down. Even Hank agreed it ranked first by a wide margin.

"I really thought one of the others would come out on top," Hank confessed later. "But the vacation lost out because Marge and I never agree with the kids on what sights to take in. The kids kind of liked the game-room idea, and it came out best on the Criterion of 'something to enjoy as much of the year as possible.' But it didn't do as well on 'something the entire family can enjoy' and 'something to help Dad relax.' I'm not much on games.

"But we do all like to swim. We could have saved a pile of money by renting a cottage; but the best beaches are three hours away, and I often have to work part of the weekend, so it would keep us apart rather than draw us together. So we decided on the pool. It had the added advantage of being a financial asset if we should decide to sell the house when the kids are in college. Frankly, I would never have gone for the idea if I hadn't seen for myself that it was the best Solution."

The family celebrated the opening of the pool the following July 4 weekend. Hank subsequently had the deck wired for sound. On summer weekends when he isn't in the office or traveling he spends time at the pool relaxing, listening to his stereo, and swimming 25 laps a day!

Let's review what happened in the above example. The Building Blocks turned a source of family contention into a cooperative search for family enjoyment. They gave Hank a way to rise above his emotional resistance to reasoned discussion. Because they involved the active participation of each member of the family, they produced a decision that each member wholeheartedly supported.

In both the swimming pool and washing machine examples, the Building Block techniques were used successfully. As you read the following example, see if you can catch Paul's mistakes in applying the Building Blocks. Here's his story, just as Paul related it to me.

"Our family of five was pretty well split over how to use my larger-than-expected Christmas bonus. One group, which I confess to being part of, felt very strongly that we should put the money toward a condominium in Florida. We had lived in Florida for several years—before the company moved me back to Cleveland—and we missed life there. We returned to Florida twice a year, at Easter and Christmas, and we felt that a condominium would be a more comfortable way to visit there.

"My wife and two daughters, on the other hand, argued that our home in Cleveland wasn't large enough, especially with my widowed mother-in-law living with us. Their idea was to build a rather sizable enclosed porch, with a bedroom for my mother-in-law at one end.

"Since nobody had any unbreakable commitments for that night, I moved everybody into the living room after dinner, took out a pad of paper, and said, 'We're going to look at this as an *opportunity*, not a problem. We're going to look at this as objectively as we can and allow no battlelines to be drawn in this room. Now, what is it we want to determine?' Everyone agreed our Purpose was to decide whether a porch or a condominium represented the best investment of our bonus.

"With our Purpose identified, I suggested we make a list of everything that might serve as a blueprint in designing our Solution. (My family was used to me talking like a draftsman, since that was my shingle for many years before I moved into manufacturing management.) I was really proud of the list that the family developed:

Achieve
Greatest benefit to the total family (both immediate family and close relatives, especially my mother-in-law)
Inflation-proof investment
Broader social life

Preserve
None

Avoid
Excessive financial commitment that would interfere with present financial obligations
Extra work for Mom and Dad as a result of the investment (my wife suggested this and I readily agreed)

"To keep things simple, I didn't discuss in any detail the concept of absolute requirements; we just listed the Criteria and then valued them with weights in a rough way. Lo and behold, when we looked at the two possible investments (condominium and porch with bedroom), they came out to a virtual tie!

"What had I done wrong? I knew that using the Building Blocks technique couldn't guarantee a clear-cut Solution, but I felt pretty bad, since the group was expecting my magic wand to produce a Solution acceptable to everyone. Instead, they felt we were no further ahead than we had been, except that it was now nine o'clock on Friday night. Teddy had missed his favorite TV program and Polly had not been able to talk with her boyfriend on the phone.

"It suddenly dawned on me that there were at least two things we should have done differently. First, in trying to save time by not determining absolute requirements, we had treated all our Criteria as desirables. So we'd missed out on an opportunity to see if one of the Alternatives should be shot down. Second, we had assumed that we could do only the porch or the condominium, whereas *maybe we could do both.* In fact, our analysis told us that we all really wanted to do both! So now we had to determine if that was financially feasible.

"Could we add a bedroom without a porch, or a porch without a bedroom? How large did the addition have to be? Where could we save money on materials and labor? Could we find a condominium that would cost less than those we had considered? Would a small house in Florida be a better investment than a condominium? We did some figuring and found that indeed we could buy a small condominium unit and furnish it, sparingly at first, while still building an addition to our Cleveland home. It's been over three years since these decisions were made, and we are delighted with both the condominium and the addition. We made a wise investment."

Although Paul and his family ultimately made the right decision, they didn't make it efficiently. Perhaps you caught their mistake right at the beginning when Paul said their Purpose was to determine whether to invest in a condominium or to add a porch with a bedroom. They would have saved themselves time and disappointment if they had recognized their true Purpose: *to determine the best way(s) to invest their bonus.*

Can the Building Blocks take the hassle out of budget and family purchase decisions? Try them and see.

# Section IV

Applying the
Building Blocks
to Personal Crises

# 15

# Marriage on the Rocks

We've learned how to apply the Seven Building Blocks to household crises and business crises. We now enter a realm where the Building Blocks may seem to have no place at all: coping with family or personal crises. Should the Building Blocks really be used in such situations? Family or personal crises, after all, involve the most sensitive of human relationships. The issues are highly emotional. The consequences of faulty judgment can be grave indeed.

If we view our lives through the spectacles of feeling and thinking, our lenses when dealing with family or personal crises would look like this:

In view of the implications of a wrong decision, isn't it best to keep the Building Blocks out of this process? Isn't professional counseling a better answer?

*Certainly, the Seven Building Blocks are no substitute for professional guidance.* My company is not, after all, in the business of marriage counseling. But precisely because they provide a structured framework for decision making, the Building Blocks can be used to help resolve complex emotional problems, either alone or in conjunction with counseling. If you decide to use them, it is essential that you clearly establish *all* your Criteria, that you weight them to reflect your true feelings and thinking, and that you consider every possible Alternative in making your analysis.

After you have done your analysis, set it aside for a few days or longer. Then reexamine it step by step to make sure it accurately reflects your best judgment. The answers you crank out are only as good as the information you crank in. You know the old saw: GIGO—garbage in, garbage out. Review your analysis from a fresh perspective. Ask a close friend, relative, or clergyman to serve as sounding board; discussing your problem and your analysis with an outsider may help you clarify your thinking. Finally, don't forget to troubleshoot. Troubleshooting a decision is doubly important when you're trying to resolve highly emotional questions under tight time pressure.

Many people have found the techniques used here helpful in dealing with personal or emotional crises. The following case histories will help you judge whether the Building Block techniques are applicable to critical emotional problems that you or a close friend may face.

Bob and Kathy Thompson both knew that their marriage was not working. It had started well enough when they met in college. He was a star athlete who turned down an offer to play professional baseball in favor of a career in marketing. She was a biology major, with ambitions of becoming a doctor. On a student tour of Europe, they fell in love. Six months later they got married. I knew them both in those days and we kept in touch for a while. I learned the story about their marriage from a mutual friend, in whom Kathy frequently confided. I later learned the details from both Bob and Kathy themselves, after running into Bob when I was called in to help his company accelerate new product development.

Kathy had given up her hopes of a career in medicine to become a wife and mother. Now, after 15 years and four children, there were only occasional glimpses of past happiness: at Christmas time; on some boisterous Saturday mornings when the younger children would jump into bed with their parents; at night when the youngest child was put to bed with lots of hugs and kisses; and on some quiet Sunday evenings when their teenage son would sit in the study and talk with his parents. What seemed to be left of the marriage was mainly the relationship with the children. Much of the time when Bob and Kathy were alone they either argued or did not talk.

Kathy saw Bob as a "workaholic" married to his job, not his wife. As director of marketing for a small consumer products company, he had been highly successful in making inroads against larger and better-financed competitors. "Because we're highly organized and are willing to work harder," he once told Kathy, "we've been known to move a newly licensed drug from the laboratory to the marketplace in half the time taken by the industry giants."

Bob took pride in his own stamina. He enjoyed working hard. He liked the challenge of beating the competition. He realized that he was frequently not available when Kathy needed him, but he felt she should be grateful that he was such a good provider and make allowances for his hectic schedule. It was, after all, his hard work that was paying for an elegant home, two late-model cars, and private schools for the children.

Kathy, however, was less than appreciative. She saw herself as abandoned, or at least relegated to third place behind Bob's career and the children. She had tried to become a realtor specializing in rural properties, but she failed the exam to get her realtor's license and appeared to lose interest in carving out a career for herself. Instead, she became heavily involved in community activities: the Girl Scouts, the church, the local hospital, the American Cancer Society. Playing bridge and smoking cigarettes became her favorite forms of relaxation.

Bob didn't find bridge relaxing. "I have to think hard all day long," he told Kathy. "The last thing in the world I want when I come home is to think hard and match my wits against other people." As for cigarettes, he did not smoke and regarded anyone who did as weak and stupid. "How can you work for the Cancer Society," he taunted, "and still smoke like a chimney? You stink up the whole house with cigarette smoke and set a terrible example for the children."

"Since when are you worried about me getting cancer?" she retorted. "You didn't worry when I was taking those damn birth control pills."

Then there were the money arguments. It was not that Bob thought Kathy spent too much money; he felt she spent money "unwisely." He accused her of buying things to impress the neighbors. It was much better, he believed, to make judicious expenditures than impressive ones. "I don't need fancy things to prove my worth," he would say. "I'm happy in blue jeans and a sweatshirt."

Eventually Kathy felt he came to resent every penny she spent. The tension took its toll. Kathy became increasingly nervous and developed severe headaches. The family doctor sent her to a specialist, who told her she was suffering from severe depression. She confessed to her friend her feelings of frustration and loneliness. "My husband," she said, "has become almost a stranger to me. We both recognize the problem, but we don't seem able to do anything about it. I think we still love each other, but I can't be sure."

Bob and Kathy underwent several months of professional counseling, separately and together. Bob recognized that his dedication to
his work was a large part of the problem. He resolved to make ad-
justments to his own lifestyle to save his marriage.

He arranged to take Kathy out to dinner once a week. It was fun at
first, but then he would find himself preoccupied and resentful of the
time away from work. He tried to tell Kathy interesting tidbits about
his job, but she wasn't interested. He also began spending more time
with his four children: Sean, 14; Jane, 10; Heather, 8; and Martin, 5.
But he often found his mind wandering after a few minutes of playing
with the kids.

"I'm just restless," he confessed to Kathy after attending a hospital
board meeting with her one night. "I guess I'm just obsessed with my
work. I know it's a failing on my part, and I'm trying to change, but it's
hard for me. I hope you can understand that."

But Kathy didn't understand, and her headaches grew worse. Bob
became increasingly concerned. He took a month off from work to take
her on a Caribbean vacation. Kathy was convinced the vacation was
Bob's way of saying, "There! You can never again say I'm not concerned about you. I have proved that I am, so never bring up the topic
again." The vacation (cost: $3,300) was pleasant, but it resolved
nothing.

The specific incident that brought the marriage into crisis was an
argument about a high school play. Bob had promised Kathy he would
go with her to see Sean perform one of the pricipal roles in the
production. He had really wanted to go. Kathy was looking forward to
an evening with her husband. She had warned him: "Now I don't want
any last-minute emergency to keep you from going to the play."

He was supposed to fly into Milwaukee from Philadelphia at 7:00
P.M., call from the airport, and meet Kathy at the school auditorium
at 7:45. The performance began at 8:00. When 7:00 came and went,
then 7:30, Kathy sensed that he was not coming. Outwardly calm but
inwardly furious, she went to the play alone. Bob still was not home
when she returned.

His secretary called her the next morning to say that he had been
delayed and would be home that night. Kathy icily thanked her for the
news. When Bob came home in the evening they had an awful fight.

"How could you be so insensitive to your own son's feelings?" she
screamed. "There he was up on stage receiving the applause of all those

people and inwardly crying because the person who meant the most to him couldn't spare the time to show up. You couldn't even call to say you couldn't make it and were sorry. What's wrong with you, Bob? Are you so wrapped in your work that you've forgotten what it is to have feelings?"

"I'm sorry," he protested. "I tried to call you, but you were already at the play. The damn jet sat on that runway in Philadelphia for an hour and 15 minutes. It had some kind of engine trouble. We finally took off and then found we couldn't land in Milwaukee because of thick fog. We circled around and around; then they rerouted us to Chicago and put us up at a motel at the airport. It was so noisy I couldn't sleep. I tried you this morning but there was no answer. What the hell was I going to do?"

"There's always some excuse. You put that damn company first and me last. You spend more time selecting Christmas gifts for your customers than for your own children. You show more consideration for your employees than you do for me."

Bob banged the table with his fist. "I'm so tired of hearing you beat on me about my work. When are you going to learn to lay off?"

On and on they went. Kathy resorted to tears. Bob resorted to silence. He picked up his bag and checked into a motel. Feeling miserable, he took a long, hot shower and asked himself what he was going to do. He had used the Building Blocks technique in business, but had never considered the possibility that they could be useful at home. Faced with the breakdown of his marriage, he said, "What the hell? What do I have to lose?"

He asked himself, "Why is any decision necessary?" (Building Block No. 1.) The answers came quickly: "I'm miserable. She's miserable. Our arguments are not good for the children. She's sick and getting sicker. I'm happier on the job than I am at home."

"So what's my Purpose?" (Building Block No. 2.) Bob tentatively decided on "determine the best way to make this marriage work." He wrote the purpose down on a piece of motel stationery.

He sent for a roast beef sandwich and a bottle of beer and settled down to work out the rest of the Building Blocks. When he scanned for Solutions, he began to have doubts about his statement of Purpose. "It's not broad enough," he thought. "It has a built-in presumption that may not be correct. Is making the marriage work really desirable for us? Could I ever become the kind of husband she expects? Would she be better off without me?"

"What's my real Purpose?" This time Bob decided on "determine the best thing to do about our marriage." He wrote that down and studied it. He liked it better than the first statement. "It's broader and it opens up more possible Solutions," he reasoned. "But for whom should I do the best thing? For me? For Kathy? For the children? I guess all of us."

Bob had the eerie feeling that he was playing God. Here he was in a strange motel trying to make a decision that would affect the lives of five people he loved, and he wasn't consulting any of them.

"Slow down," he told himself. "You have to build in Criteria for Kathy and the children. What do *we* want to achieve, preserve, and avoid? Certainly we want the confidence of the children; we want to resolve the cause of our arguments; we want a more positive lease on life. We want to preserve our image in the community, preserve our own self-image, and preserve the marriage. We want to avoid hatred and bitterness, any adverse effect on my job performance, and aggravation of Kathy's health problems (whether they are real or imaginary, mental or physical). And we certainly want to avoid scandal of any type, or even rumors of one."

Bob knew that he was not in any condition to reach a Solution that night, but at least he felt he was using his emotions constructively. Before going to bed, he listed five possible Solutions: divorce, separation, continuation of the marriage in the present state, improving the marriage through counseling, and establishing a career for his wife. None of them excited him; in fact, he found himself depressed after listing them. Wasn't there an "innovative" Alternative?

He thought for a minute and added a sixth: developing a relationship outside the marriage. He had never sought the companionship of another woman, but he felt that he surely needed an emotional outlet now. The idea of another woman intrigued him but also filled him with guilt. Was this a way of trying to punish Kathy? Did he need another woman to add to his problems? How would he go about finding one? He felt ludicrous! It worried him too. He shrugged and put a question mark after it. Then, encouraged that he had made a beginning, he turned out the light. His list, when he went to sleep, looked like this:

## PURPOSE

Determine the best thing to do about our marriage

## CRITERIA

Achieve
  Children's confidence
  End to constant arguments
  More positive lease on life for Kathy and me

Preserve
  Image in community
  Self-image
  Marriage

Avoid
  Hatred and bitterness
  Adverse effect on job performance
  Aggravating Kathy's health problems
  Scandal or rumors

## POSSIBLE SOLUTIONS

  Divorce
  Separation
  Continuation of status quo
  Marriage plus counseling
  Marriage plus establishing career for Kathy
  Marriage plus another woman

After work the next day he slowly drove home. At first Kathy behaved as though nothing had happened. But after the children were in bed the recriminations began

"Will you explain to me why nothing I say ever counts?" she said. "You get your way all the time and I have to submit. Even when we first met, in Europe, you wanted to go to Spain and I wanted to go to Paris. Where did we go? Spain. To this day I haven't seen Paris. If we go to the movies and I want to see *The Sound of Music*, you take me to see Ingmar Bergman. If we spend an evening at home listening to stereo tapes and I want to hear Sigmund Romberg, do I get him?  No. You cram Stravinsky down my throat. Why do you always come first and I always come last?"

Bob started to deny her charges, then he thought, "She's right. I have had my way in almost everything." Aloud he said, "I guess we are different kinds of people. What is important to you is not as important to me, and what is important to me is not as important to you."

"I'm glad to hear you admit it. For a minute I thought you were going to deny it." She said good night and went upstairs to bed, leaving him in the living room, alone with his thoughts.

Bob got out his Building Block analysis. He thought of asking Kathy to discuss it with him, but he reasoned that their relationship was too strained for that. He began refining the Criteria. He combined some Criteria and expanded others. Then he turned to setting Priorities.

Were there any absolute requirements? Yes. Whatever he did he would have to be able to live with it in good conscience. What about Kathy's health?  Should an absolute requirement be to avoid aggravating her health problems or triggering a possible nervous breakdown? No, he decided, for three reasons. First, there could be no guarantee that any Solution would safeguard Kathy's health. Second, making her health an absolute requirement might make any Solution impossible. Finally, he concluded, his decision should be made for the welfare of the whole family, not just Kathy.

But safeguarding Kathy's health was an important objective. He ranked it as the most important among his desirable objectives, with a value of 10. The second most important objective, he decided, should be to "permit both of us to function effectively." That received an 8. Then it occurred to him that the objective had two parts: Kathy's functioning effectively, which he gave a 5, and his own functioning effectively, which he gave a 3. (He reasoned that Kathy would find it more difficult to adjust to a change in their relationship than he would.)

As for the kids, he decided what he really wanted was to "minimize the adverse impact of whatever we do." He rated it a 7. It was important but slightly less so than his and Kathy's ability to function. (Kathy, he reasoned, had to be able to function effectively to raise them, and he would have to function effectively to support them.) "Preserving the marriage," which had started out as his statement of Purpose, was now reduced to a desirable objective with a value of 4. That was as it should be, he thought, because preserving Kathy's health was more than twice as important, and preserving their image in the community was only half as important.

When he reviewed his Solutions, Bob realized that two of them had already been tried: improving the marriage through counseling and establishing a career for Kathy. He crossed them out. It was true that Kathy had talked about wanting to take the realtor's exam again; a friend had even told her that if she got her license he'd take her into his real estate agency. But Bob was convinced she would never overcome her headaches and nervousness and be able to embark on a career as long as she remained married to him.

He thought of another Solution: accommodating his own lifestyle and values to hers. "Can I be more attentive? Hell, I've tried that. Should I get another job? I'd be the same on any job. The trouble is I'm set in my ways and probably can't change dramatically. The things that she values I don't, and the things I value she doesn't. We've just gone in different directions."

When Bob tallied his Solutions, he found divorce the best choice by a margin of almost 40 percent. Separation ranked second, and preserving the status quo third. He was relieved to find that another woman emerged as the worst Solution. Bob's analysis is shown in Chart L.

V = value
R = rating

## CHART L    Purpose: Determine the best thing to do about our marriage

| CRITERIA | | ALTERNATIVE A Separation | | | ALTERNATIVE B Divorce | | | ALTERNATIVE C Status Quo | | | ALTERNATIVE D C Plus Relationship with Another Woman | | |
|---|---|---|---|---|---|---|---|---|---|---|---|---|---|
| Absolute Requirements | | Yes | | | Yes | | | Yes | | | Very doubtful | | |
| Something I can do in good conscience | | | | | | | | | | | | | |
| Desirable Objectives | | | R | V × R | | R | V × R | | R | V × R | | R | V × R |
| V | | | | | | | | | | | | | |
| 10 | Avoid aggravating Kathy's health problems/possible nervous breakdown | Further uncertainty may well aggravate health problems | 5 | 50 | More secure status than A; guarantee financial security | 10 | 100 | Headed toward breakdown now | 2 | 20 | May trigger breakdown if Kathy finds out | 0 | 0 |
| 8 | Preserve/improve ability to function effectively | Will either start new life or cling to old | 5 | 25 | Clear break with me should free her to start new life | 10 | 50 | Continued aggravation, tension, dependency | 2 | 10 | If she doesn't discover better than C, if she does, worse than C | 3 | 15 |
| (5) | Kathy's ability | | | | | | | | | | | | |
| (3) | My ability | Okay, but continued strains | 7 | 21 | Better, clearer definition of my obligations | 10 | 30 | Continued aggravation, tension | 3 | 9 | Might make me easier to live with but no long-term stability | 5 | 15 |
| 7 | Minimize adverse impact on kids | Kids may feel rejected, uncertain, but less day-to-day stress than now | 4 | 28 | May feel rejected, but should improve as they come to accept change | 10 | 70 | Kids are suffering and will get worse | 3 | 21 | Kids will feel rejected and betrayed | 0 | 0 |
| 6 | Minimize bitterness between Kathy and me | Bitterness will be less than C and D | 7 | 42 | Will be bitterness, should improve with new relationship | 10 | 60 | Bitterness will get worse | 3 | 18 | Bitterness will be awful if she discovers; if she doesn't, little change | 2 | 12 |
| 5 | Provide long-term resolution/stability of situation | Interim measure | 5 | 25 | Definitely | 10 | 50 | Highly doubtful | 0 | 0 | No | 0 | 0 |
| 4 | Preserve worthwhile marriage | Some chance if absence brings about reconciliation | 5 | 20 | No chance | 0 | 0 | Best doesn't find out | 10 | 40 | Some chance if she doesn't find out | 7 | 28 |
| 2 | Preserve image in community (family, friends, business associates, customers) | Second best, but not good (rumors, loss of respect) | 5 | 10 | Second worse (may be rumors) | 2 | 4 | Best | 10 | 20 | Worst | 1 | 2 |
| TOTAL POINTS | | | 221 | | THE WINNER | 364 | | | 138 | | | 72 | |

Instead of feeling exhilarated by his Solution, Bob began to feel increasingly uneasy as he studied his analysis. Something in his gut told him it was wrong. He rechecked his Criteria, then rechecked his ratings and the reasons for them. Everything seemed right—except the totals. "Divorce might be the best Solution," he mumbled to himself. "But almost 40 percent better? It couldn't be. Something is wrong. Maybe I need to forget it for a few days and then try again." He folded up his chart, put it in his briefcase, and tiptoed upstairs to bed. Kathy hadn't even left the night light on for him.

Bob and Kathy hardly spoke during the next few days. She was asleep when he left for work each morning. Because of an extremely heavy workload, he had to work late several evenings and found her asleep when he got home. The one evening that he had dinner with the family was uneventful.

The following week Bob was away on business. He called home twice and chatted with each of the kids. He exchanged a few words with Kathy, making it a point to tell her he hoped things were going well. She said everything was all right. "I'm getting used to fending for myself," she said offhandedly.

The night before he was to return home Bob reviewed his chart, then put it aside and began a new one. His Criteria were identical, as were the values he assigned to them. But when he began listing Alternatives, he decided to include the two he had previously rejected: "continuing the marriage with counseling" and "continuing the marriage while helping Kathy establish a career."

He restored "continuing the marriage with counseling" because Kathy had thought the counseling was doing some good; it was *his* schedule that had interfered with the sessions. He restored "continuing the marriage while helping Kathy establish a career" because Kathy had begun talking about taking the realtor's exam again. During one recent fight she bluntly said: "I'd rather stand on my own two feet than be stood up by you."

"It's worth examining how they both stack up," he reasoned. This time Bob decided against restricting himself to a single numerical weight in evaluating each Alternative against each Criterion. For example, if Kathy *could* develop a career for herself, that Alternative would score highest on the Criterion of "preserve/improve her ability to function." But could she? He concluded that a single standard was inadequate to make the required comparisons, because it couldn't measure both the *likelihood* of something happening and the *impact* if it did happen.

Instead, he used a measure consisting of two numbers, a minimum and a maximum for each Alternative. Under this min/max system, the

Alternative of a career for Kathy rated a 4/10 against the Criterion of "preserve/improve her ability to function": 4 at worst (if a career didn't work out for her) and 10 at best (if it did). It was, he reasoned, still an imperfect standard of measurement but more refined than a single-number system. He then averaged the min/max for each Alternative and compared the averages. Chart M shows Bob's second analysis.

Bob compared the totals three ways, as follows:

| | Alternative | At Worst | At Best | Average |
|---|---|---|---|---|
| A | Separation | 78 | 195 | (78 + 195)/2 = 136.5 |
| B | Divorce | 156 | 270 | (156 + 270)/2 = 213.0 |
| C | Status quo | 37 | 165 | (37 + 165)/2 = 101.0 |
| D | Marriage plus another woman | 23 | 101 | (23 + 101)/2 = 62.0 |
| E | Marriage plus counseling | 153 | 399 | (153 + 399)/2 = 276.0 |
| F | Marriage plus career for Kathy | 129 | 413 | (129 + 413)/2 = 271.0 |

Alternatives E and F came out significantly better than the others on both the At Best and the Average scales. On the At Worst scale, E came out statistically tied with B; F was 10 percent behind. Overall, it was a clear win for E and F.

He copied the Average scores in descending order of importance, as follows:

| | Alternative | Average |
|---|---|---|
| E | Marriage plus counseling | 276.0 |
| F | Marriage plus career for Kathy | 271.0 |
| B | Divorce | 213.0 |
| A | Separation | 136.5 |
| C | Status quo | 101.0 |
| D | Marriage plus another woman | 62.0 |

As he reviewed the totals, Bob found himself elated for the first time in weeks. Marriage plus counseling, which ranked first, and marriage plus a career for Kathy, which was a close second, were far and away the highest-scoring Solutions, more than 20 percent "better" than divorce, which ranked third. The others trailed so badly that they

V = value
W/B = at worst/at best

# CHART M    Purpose: Determine the best thing to do about our marriage

| CRITERIA | ALTERNATIVE A Separation | | | ALTERNATIVE B Divorce | | | ALTERNATIVE C Status Quo | | |
|---|---|---|---|---|---|---|---|---|---|
| | | W/B | V × W/B | | W/B | V × W/B | | W/B | V × W/B |
| **Absolute Requirements** | | | | | | | | | |
| Something I can do in good conscience | Yes, but might feel guilty; long period of uncertainty for family pending decision | | | Yes, if necessary | | | Can I keep on this way? Yes, if I thought it would all end well | | |
| **V    Desirable Objectives** | | | | | | | | | |
| 10  Avoid aggravating Kathy's health problem/possible nervous breakdown breakdown | Difficult, would have guilt; must not go on too long | 3/6 | 30/60 | Could aggravate, but once it's a fact, she can adjust to it | 5/7 | 50/70 | Bad the way we're heading | 2/6 | 20/60 |
| 8    Preserve/improve ability to function effectively | | | | | | | | | |
| 5    (5) Kathy's ability | Should once resolution made | 3/6 | 15/30 | Should as initial shock wears off | 6/8 | 30/40 | Bad—living in limbo | 1/4 | 5/20 |
| (3) My ability | Difficult at first but can accommodate | 3/6 | 9/18 | Will free me from some frustration and guilt | 4/7 | 12/21 | Could drag me down increasingly | 1/5 | 3/15 |
| 7    Minimize adverse impact on kids | Limbo—they'd keep hoping I'd come back | 1/4 | 7/28 | Once a fait accompli, they'd accept it | 4/7 | 28/49 | Rough and will probably get rougher on them | 1/4 | 7/28 |
| 6    Minimize bitterness between Kathy and me | Difficult—the longer, the harder! | 1/3 | 6/18 | Once done, we may remain friends | 1/5 | 6/30 | Increase bitterness | 0/4 | 0/24 |
| 5    Provide long-term resolution/ stability of situation | Doesn't; an interim measure | 1/1 | 5/5 | Okay if no recriminations | 4/10 | 20/50 | Bad! | 0/0 | 0/0 |
| 4    Preserve worthwhile marriage | Doubtful we'd get back together on a worthwhile bases but possible | 1/7 | 4/28 | That's the end! | 0/0 | 0/0 | Probably get worse | 0/4 | 0/16 |
| 2    Preserve image in community (family, friends, business associates, customers) | No. Awkward; people may wonder and gossip | 1/4 | 2/8 | Yes, if explained and image preserved | 5/5 | 10/10 | Bound to deteriorate; her friends think I'm a bastard already! | 1/1 | 2/2 |
| TOTAL POINTS | | | 78/195 | | | 156/270 | | | 37/165 |

## CHART M (continued)

| CRITERIA | ALTERNATIVE D — C Plus Relationship with Another Woman | | | ALTERNATIVE E — C Plus Counseling | | | ALTERNATIVE F — C Plus Career for Kathy | | |
|---|---|---|---|---|---|---|---|---|---|
| **Absolute Requirements** | | W/B | V × W/B | | W/B | V × W/B | | W/B | V × W/B |
| Something I can do in good conscience | Possible? Married to my business; maybe woman would make better "mistress"! | | | Sure; no conscience problem in trying again | | | Same as E | | |
| **V   Desirable Objectives** | | | | | | | | | |
| 10  Avoid aggravating Kathy's health problem/possible nervous breakdown | Bad, if she found out or even suspected | 0/2 | 0/20 | Good if it works; bad if it doesn't; hopeful anyway | 5/10 | 50/100 | If this proved feasible, great; if not, serious disappointment | 3/10 | 30/100 |
| 8  Preserve/improve ability to function effectively | | | | | | | | | |
| (5) Kathy's ability | Okay if she could hate me and could justify my actions | 3/6 | 15/30 | Best if successful; if not? | 4/10 | 20/50 | Also looks very good—if it works! | 3/10 | 35/50 |
| (3) My ability | If I could find this acceptable, could help; but probability? | 1/6 | 3/18 | If it works, great! If not, worse off than now? | 3/9 | 9/27 | If it works, I'd be freer; if it doesn't? | 4/10 | 12/30 |
| 7  Minimize adverse impact on kids | She would never understand | 0/2 | 0/14 | Kids' hopes up; great if it works out, but it may not! | 3/10 | 21/70 | Great if it works out, but would kids feel neglected? | 3/9 | 21/63 |
| 6  Minimize bitterness between Kathy and me | When she found out, watch out! | 0/0 | 0/0 | Okay if it works out; If not, "at least we tried" | 4/9 | 24/54 | Great if it works out; if not? | 3/10 | 18/60 |
| 5  Provide long-term resolution/stability of situation | Doubtful it could lead to resolution and stability | 1/3 | 5/15 | Could be best; if it doesn't work out, no worse off than now | 3/10 | 15/50 | Could be good, but if not? | 3/10 | 15/50 |
| 4  Preserve worthwhile marriage | Doubtful | 0/1 | 0/4 | Maybe yes, maybe no | 2/9 | 8/36 | Could give her sense of self-worth now lacking, but if it fails? | 3/10 | 12/40 |
| 2  Preserve image in community (family, friends, business associates, customers) | No way! Recriminations | 0/0 | 0/0 | Some scuttlebut bound to occur; awkward | 3/6 | 6/12 | Best, if it works; if not? | 3/10 | 6/20 |
| **TOTAL POINTS** | | | 23/101 | | | 153/399 | | | 149/413 |

didn't appear worthy of serious consideration. Again, marriage plus another woman fared the worst.

He unfolded the old chart and compared the answers on the two sheets. It was hard to believe the same person had filled out both charts. The first was the work of a man disillusioned with marriage; the second, of a man who still had the will to make marriage work. Which was the real Bob Thompson? He sat back and thought about himself and his own attitude. He had never allowed himself to feel defeated at work. Why should he feel defeated at home? Maybe these problems couldn't be worked out, but damn it he was going to try. His excitement told him that he still loved Kathy. He returned home elated.

Kathy didn't seem particularly happy to see him. She rarely did. But she noticed that for once Bob seemed glad to be home. He made jokes with the kids at dinner. He told a hilarious story that even made her laugh. After the kids were in bed, he poured her a glass of her favorite sherry, then one for himself. "You never drink sherry. Has something changed?" she asked.

"Something in me has changed," he said. He explained his soul searching of the past two weeks. He brought out the two charts and explained them to her step by step. "I almost decided to call it quits last week," he confessed, "but something told me it would be wrong. And I knew it for sure when I saw how excited I was seeing the results of the second chart." He added, "Honey, I want to do all I can to make this marriage work. I'll do my part. I'll even do more than my part. I hope you will try too."

Kathy listened to him attentively but without enthusiasm. When he had finished, there was a long pause. Then she spoke. "I agree with everything you've said, Bob. We've made an awful mess of things. It won't be easy to repair the damage. I'm not as optimistic as you are. But I'm willing to try again. I guess we have nothing to lose by trying."

At this writing Bob and Kathy have been faithfully going to a psychiatrist for several months. Their marriage seems to be slowly on the mend. Kathy is studying for her realtor's exam again. Her headaches have not disappeared but they are less frequent. Bob still travels frequently on business. But when he's in town, he makes it a point to be home for dinner three nights a week. He and Kathy have a theater subscription (he would have preferred the symphony) and dine out one night a week. Kathy has begun giving small dinner parties; as many of *her* friends are invited as *his*.

Their problems aren't over. But their situation is much improved.

"The big thing," says Kathy, "is that we're communicating for the first time in years."

Another couple in the same circumstances may have resolved this marriage problem differently. There is no right or wrong Solution. What is important is that the Solution best suits the needs and wants of the parties involved.

Using the Building Blocks to help resolve a personal crisis may strike you as inappropriate. In my view, it isn't—*if you are sure that the values you assign to your Priorities and Alternatives truly reflect both your thinking and your feelings.* The key is in the balance:

In resolving highly personal problems, there are certain rules that should be followed. Always make sure that your values and ratings represent your true thinking and feeling. If you have doubts—as Bob did—after you've arrived at a Solution put your analysis aside for a few days. Try to find a sounding board to help you sort out your feelings and your options. It's easier to clarify your values by talking things over than by working alone. If at all possible, work through the problem with the people who will be affected. Shared Solutions are preferable to solo Solutions.

Make sure you've considered all the Alternatives, even the improbable ones (in Bob's case, developing a relationship with another woman). Then troubleshoot your decision and think through how best to make your announcement (in what setting, in what words). Foresight will eliminate any need for hindsight. Finally, consider seeking professional guidance, particularly if the issues involve or are likely to cause severe emotional problems.

# 16

## To Be or Not to Be a Mother

Sue Parsons was 18, a senior in high school, and nine months pregnant.

She was short—about 5'3"—and my first impression of her as she walked into my office was of strength and of browns: deep brown eyes; straight brown hair; a brown coat to shut out the winter cold. Despite some obvious discomfort, she moved with a sense of grace and determination. She had participated in a series of youth workshops where she had learned about using the Building Blocks to solve personal crises. An only child who lived with her parents, she had dropped out of school to avoid embarrassment over her pregnancy. She had been tutored for the last few months and hoped to graduate with her class.

Sue sat now with her hands folded, calmly describing her situation. The baby was due in just three weeks; her relationships with her parents and her boyfriend were strained; her future was up for grabs. Yet she gave every appearance of having complete control over her life. Was she on drugs? Was she a consummate actress? Was she cracking up inside with a thin shell of self-confidence holding her together? These questions crossed my mind as I listened to her predicament.

She loved her parents but had trouble accepting many of their ways. She had been raised a Catholic but now considered herself an agnostic. Her lack of faith was a source of conflict with her parents. She had been seeing her boyfriend, Phil, for two years. She thought she loved him and wanted to marry him. But she wasn't sure. "I'm just not ready to be tied down," she kept saying.

Sue's dream was to become a biochemist. An excellent student, she had been offered a grant by the American Field Service (AFS) to study abroad for a year. If she accepted it, there was a good chance she could get a scholarship to a four-year college. She felt she could leave Phil for the year without damaging their relationship. In fact, she felt that the year apart would strengthen their bond by making them want each other more.

Against her dream of becoming a biochemist were the plans held out for her by her parents and her boyfriend. And overriding these considerations was her uncertainty about what to do with the baby. Whenever she mentioned the baby, she became uneasy. She sighed, bit her lip, then turned to another subject.

Sue's parents wanted her to become a nurse. If they had their way, she said, she would go to nursing school, marry a doctor, and bear them grandchildren. They were sure that Sue would outgrow her desire for both biochemistry and Phil. The Parsons were pressuring Sue to put the baby up for adoption, forget about travel and a career in biochemistry, and attend a nearby junior college to study nursing. They were willing to pay for the two-year school but felt that a four-year liberal arts education would be "wasted on a girl."

Phil saw value in Sue's ambitions to become a biochemist but thought she should postpone them. He wanted to get married right away and give the baby "a proper home." Phil was 20 and worked part time to support himself while studying to become an X-ray technician. He loved Sue and depended on her to provide a measure of stability that had been lacking in his own life. The product of a broken home, Phil had grown up without knowing who his father was. He was, Sue admitted, "immature in a lot of ways."

After we had talked for almost two hours, I thought that Sue might be tired. I suggested we arrange to meet again in a few days. But the thought of stopping upset her. She started picking at her nails. She said she didn't want to come back in a couple of days; she wanted to talk now.

"I came to you because I thought you could help me decide what to do. I need some help now." She started to cry. "I feel like I'm being torn in 20 different directions," she said. "My parents want me to give up the baby and become a nurse. Phil wants me to keep the baby and marry him. I want to travel and have a career. But I don't know what to do about the baby, or my parents, or Phil. I need to know what to do."

I gulped and mentally juggled my timetable. "Okay, Sue. We'll take as much time as we need," I said. As she composed herself, I realized why she had appeared so calm: she was sure that by the end of the day everything would be sorted out. "Let's be clear about one thing," I continued. "There are *no* perfect answers. I'll help you decide the best Solution for you, but it won't solve all your problems."

She said she understood.

"Now, it seems to me, Sue, that you have a number of different problems, all interrelated. We have to separate them in order to manage them." She nodded her head in agreement.

"Okay, would you agree the most pressing problem is what to do about the baby?"

"Yes, I would."

"Let me get down on paper some of the others." I produced the following list:

What should you do about the baby?

What should you do about the scholarship abroad?

What should you do about Phil's pressure to marry?

How responsible do you feel for Phil?

What, if any, moral support do you need from your parents?

What financial support do you need from your parents?

Sue sighed at the long list.

"Depressed?" I asked.

"In a way, yes, but it feels good to be able to share these problems. I've been carrying them for so long alone," she said.

She excused herself to go the ladies' room. I quickly huddled with my secretary to rearrange my schedule so I could continue to help Sue. When she returned, I said, "Now let's take up the most pressing problem, the baby." It was due in three weeks. Only a few days after delivery, Sue would have to decide whether to put it up for adoption. If she made up her mind right now, she could begin to relax.

We discussed what she wanted to achieve, preserve, and avoid by any decision she made. Our list read like this:

## PURPOSE
Determine the best thing to do about the baby

## CRITERIA
Achieve
  Education in biochemistry
  Self-support
  Personal growth

Preserve
  Assurance that the baby is in good hands
  Relationship with Phil
  Relationship with parents

Avoid
   Being forced into nursing
   Being pressured into marrying Phil

I showed her the list and asked her which Criteria were most important. Were there any absolute requirements, conditions that would have to be met no matter what she decided?

She said, "Well, I don't think I'm ready to marry Phil yet."

"Anything else?"

"No, I don't think so."

"That's okay. We're making progress," I said.

Sue nodded.

We went over the remaining Criteria, giving reasons for them and attaching values to them. Here's how Sue ranked them:

   10   Obtain an education in biochemistry, starting with the AFS scholarship ("because that's my chosen field and the best way to pursue it")
   10   Make sure that the baby is in good hands ("so that it can have a good home and I can avoid feeling guilty about putting my life ahead of the baby's)
   8   Avoid being forced into nursing ("because I have no interest in this field at all")
   7   Achieve personal growth ("in order to be a well-rounded individual")
   5   Preserve my relationship with Phil ("because I do like—love—him and would probably marry him after graduating from college")
   3   Support myself ("but I wouldn't mind being supported by scholarships as long as I could obtain a good education")

We next formed a matrix and listed the Criteria on the left-hand side, with their respective values. We identified the options open to her as follows:

## POSSIBLE SOLUTIONS

   Put baby up for adoption
   Let parents bring up baby
   Keep baby myself
   Marry Phil and bring up baby together
   Live with Phil and bring up baby together

In rating the Alternatives against the Criteria, Sue seemed to be talking out of both sides of her mouth. On the one hand, she said that she felt having responsibility for the baby—even if the baby lived with her parents—would limit her development. She also said her parents didn't like Phil and might try to force him out of the picture. On the other hand, she argued that Phil understood her need for development and would help out if they took up housekeeping together, "so the baby wouldn't be that much of a problem."

I was a little surprised that she hadn't set as an absolute Criterion "assuring that the baby is in good hands." But she reiterated that the most important thing was to avoid marriage. "I just feel that I have the potential to make a contribution in this world. Even though it may be selfish, getting my education is as important to me as seeing to it that the baby has a good home."

After we completed our chart, I totaled the results and showed them to Sue. Putting the baby up for adoption came out first. It scored 23 percent higher than leaving the baby with her parents, which ranked second. Living with Phil and bringing up the baby together ranked third, and bringing up the baby herself ranked last. Chart N shows Sue's analysis.

Sue studied the chart for several minutes, then said, "I feel relieved in a way. But I also feel guilty. How am I going to feel five years from now when I remember that somewhere in this world I have a baby and I don't even know where? And how will I feel if Phil and I drift apart?"

"Sue," I said, "I can't guarantee you won't feel guilty about the baby in five years. But think how you might feel if you brought up the baby and couldn't get an education. Would you have some hostile feelings? Would you feel that you'd missed out on something? A reputable adoption agency will see to it that the baby is placed in an excellent home. Is this something you might want to investigate? As for your relationship with Phil, you rated preserving it only half as important as getting an education. If it's more important to you than that, let's redo the chart. But if the chart accurately reflects your values, are you truly willing to accept the possibility that you and Phil may drift apart?"

Sue reexamined the chart for a long time, then put it down and stared out the window. "I think the chart really does show where I'm at. I've tried too hard to please him, at the expense of what I really think *I* want out of life. It will be hard on Phil if I go away. Maybe I can discuss my decision with him so it won't hurt him so much."

Because her decision affected both Phil and her parents, I suggested that she return the next day to discuss how to gain their understanding and support. I wanted to give her a chance to think over her decision and to make sure it really did represent her best judgment. If it did, I wanted to help her troubleshoot what could go wrong and take preventive action. But we had done enough for one day; I could see

V = value
R = rating

## CHART N    Purpose: Determine the best thing to do about the baby

| CRITERIA | ALTERNATIVE A Put Baby Up For Adoption | | | ALTERNATIVE B Let Parents Bring Up Baby | | | ALTERNATIVE C Keep Baby | | | ALTERNATIVE D Marry Phil and Bring Baby Up Together | ALTERNATIVE E Live with Phil and Bring Baby Up Together | | |
|---|---|---|---|---|---|---|---|---|---|---|---|---|---|
| **Absolute Requirements** | | | | | | | | | | | | | |
| Avoid marriage with Phil now | Yes | | | Yes | | | Yes | | | No | Yes | | |
| | R | V×R | | R | V×R | | R | V×R | | | R | V×R | |
| **V  Desirable Objectives** | | | | | | | | | | | | | |
| 10  Make sure baby is in good hands | High probability of good home but no assurance | 8 | 80 | Very stable home; lots of love | 10 | 100 | Tough living alone and going back to school or work | 3 | 30 | | Real struggle; advantage of father—but how stable is Phil? | 4 | 40 |
| 10  Obtain education in Biochemistry | No obstacle | 10 | 100 | Parents might influence my actions, but I won't be tied down | 6 | 60 | Tied down; hard to pursue career | 2 | 20 | | Less tied down; Phil could help with baby, but still hard | 3 | 30 |
| 8  Avoid being forced into nursing | No chance | 10 | 80 | Parental influence | 5 | 40 | Easy to avoid | 8 | 64 | | Easy to avoid | 8 | 64 |
| 7  Achieve personal growth | No obstacle | 10 | 70 | Obligation to be near baby may limit me | 5 | 35 | Very limiting | 2 | 14 | | Less limiting if Phil shares | 4 | 28 |
| 5  Preserve relationship with Phil | Removes baby as bond; will anger him | 1 | 5 | Parents may ease Phil out of picture | 4 | 20 | Phil will feel responsible | 8 | 40 | | We'll be a family | 10 | 50 |
| 3  Obtain self-support | No obstacle | 10 | 30 | Little obstacle | 8 | 24 | Large obstacle | 2 | 6 | | Less obstacle than C | 4 | 12 |
| TOTAL POINTS | THE WINNER | | 365 | | | 279 | | | 174 | | | | 224 |

that Sue was exhausted from the strain of our discussion. And so was I!

Before setting an appointment for the following afternoon, I urged Sue not to make a final decision until she had consulted with a reputable adoption agency. I gave her the names of several to try.

She never returned. Instead, she called to say she'd had long talks with her parents and Phil. Her parents were pleased that she'd decided to give up the baby, but they were sure a year in Europe would be a waste of time. Phil was upset about her plans for the baby and for her education. Sue said that there was no point in her taking up more of my time since everything had been decided. She thanked me profusely. I protested that I would be glad to talk to her further. She said she'd try to come in again, but she never did.

Sue had her baby, and it was adopted. She graduated with her class and went abroad to study in the fall. She saw Phil from time to time before she left, but their relationship cooled after she gave up the baby. Her parents remained puzzled by their daughter, wanting her to become someone she would never be.

I'm convinced that Sue's decision was the right one for her. Someone holding a different set of values, of course, would have come to a different conclusion. I'm also convinced that she could have done a better job of winning over her parents and her boyfriend if she had thought through how to explain her decision—or even better, if she had involved her parents and Phil in the decision. Of course, she might not have succeeded. But had she tried to anticipate the pitfalls of her decision and acted positively before they occurred, it would have been easier for her and perhaps for her parents and Phil too.

Sue's example points out the benefit of having a sounding board—a trusted, sensitive, and supportive person—to help you sort out conflicting personal feelings. Such a person should draw out your thoughts and feelings without imposing his or her value system on you. Had I, for example, sought to inflict my personal values on Sue, I would have done her an injustice. By raising questions in an atmosphere of understanding and confidentiality, I was able to help her *feel* and *think* her way to a Solution that she believed best reconciled her personal ambition with her sense of obligation toward the baby, her parents, and the father of her child.

Sue's case also demonstrates the value of the Building Blocks in resolving personal crises. This technique for decision making focused her attention on the question of most pressing importance, structured her search for a Solution, and gave her—after months of inner turmoil—the assurance she needed to carry out in good conscience the decision she made.

# Section V

## Clarifying Your Career Ambitions; Planning Your Life Goals

# 17

# Job and Life Planning

A few years ago one of my associates was asked to give a talk on career planning to 30 teenagers who belonged to a church youth group. He began by handing a sheet of paper to each of the youths and asking them to write down the job or jobs that most appealed to them. Then he told them to put the lists away.

Next he asked them to describe what they wanted in a job. When he had written down their answers on the blackboard, he asked for suggestions on what they *didn't* want in a job. He ended up with this rather amateurish list of Criteria—things to achieve, preserve, and avoid:

Achieve
    Working with people
    Solving problems
    Becoming famous
    Having power
    Being able to give orders
    Allowing plenty of time for family or hobbies
    Traveling
    Helping people
    Becoming rich
    Becoming comfortable
    Being happy

Preserve
    Good health
    Feeling of accomplishment

Good family life
Time to enjoy life

Avoid
Constant worries
Working too hard
Uninteresting work
Low pay

My associate then handed out another piece of paper and asked the youths to write down the things that they personally wanted to achieve, preserve, and avoid in any career they entered. He asked them to rank the qualities in order of importance. He said that they needn't restrict themselves to the Criteria listed on the blackboard.

Then he had them take out the original list of jobs that appealed to them most and compare it with the list of things they wanted to achieve, preserve, and avoid in a career. The results were astonishing. Many of the young people were attracted to careers that contradicted their strongest objectives. One youngster in his late teens, for example, said he wanted to become a teacher. But his primary objective was to "become rich." Another young man said that he wanted to travel. Yet the job that appealed to him most was that of a fireman.

The exercise, crude as it was, demonstrates an important point in choosing careers or changing jobs: you must start with your objectives. Only after you have clearly defined them can you consider occupations that will satisfy them.

The point was driven home to me one night in San Francisco when I looked up an old friend who was searching for work. Hugh had asked me to dinner at his home. He picked me up at my hotel. Before leaving, we stopped in the bar for a drink and played the usual old-friend guessing game: "Whatever happened to so and so?" Gradually the talk turned to Hugh and his job search.

"What kind of job are you looking for?" I asked.
"I don't know exactly. But something that I can excel at. I really want to make my mark on the world," he said earnestly.

By the time the evening was over, Hugh had discovered—through the Building Blocks—that his Purpose was actually quite different.

Six weeks earlier Hugh had quit his job as a fund raiser for a major university in a dispute with his boss. His wife, Joanne, had been very upset about his abrupt departure from the university. Before taking that job, Hugh had spent four years as a freelance composer. He had started off with a hit single that made him over $25,000, but then things got tight. In his last three years as a full-time composer he had earned a total of only $18,000. It had been a rough time for Joanne. Things had improved with the university job, which paid $12,000 per year. The couple had bought a small house and spent months fixing it up themselves.

In the six weeks since his last paycheck Hugh had become discouraged about finding a job as good as the one he'd given up. But now, suddenly, he had been offered two jobs: both in fund raising, both within commuting distance of his home, and both offering more money than the one he quit. There was only one hitch: he had to make up his mind by Wednesday morning. And here it was Monday evening.

What should he do? Joanne was afraid both job offers would fall through because of her husband's indecision. In her view, any steady job was better than freelance work. She couldn't understand why he was agonizing over the choice.

"Why *are* you agonizing?" I asked.

"Because I want to make sure I choose the job that's best for the next four or five years."

We finished our drinks, got in Hugh's car, and sped along the Bay Shore Freeway toward his home.

"My choice would be easier if both jobs didn't sound so damn good," said Hugh. He explained that one was with a college, at $16,000 a year, the other with a museum, at $18,000.

"At the college I'd be working for the director of development, who is an able man. There are many other small colleges in the country, so my experience would be applicable in a lot of other places. On the other hand, the pay, though good, is not great. I'd be one of several staff members, and fund-raising work offers less opportunity at a small college than at a university."

"What about the museum offer?"

"Well, there I'd be director of development, the head man in fund raising. And I would report to the director of the museum. I'd have greater responsibility, with better pay, and I'd be in charge of several volunteers. But I'd have no paid staff members to work with, and the museum has some big financial problems. Still, I could truly make a contribution to the museum by helping to put it on a firmer financial base."

Hugh continued to discuss the pros and cons of the college and the museum jobs, examining the variables like different-colored balls, mentally throwing one ball in the air while he picked up another.

When he turned into his driveway, he seemed exhausted from his juggling act—and no closer to a decision.

We were greeted at the door by Joanne and their daughter, Michele, 15. Declining our offer to help prepare dinner, they disappeared into the kitchen. We poured ourselves a drink and continued our discussion.

"From what you've said thus far, Hugh, it seems to me that your Purpose is to determine which job offers the better opportunity for you to make a mark on the world. I think that's how you put it at the hotel. Does that sound right?"

"Very definitely," he responded.

Rather than weigh the pros and cons, I asked him to tell me all the things he'd like to *achieve* in any job he took, all the things he'd like to *preserve*, and all the things he'd like to *avoid*. I also suggested that, rather than restrict himself to discussing the college and the museum offers, he pretend he hadn't received any offers. If he thought only about what he wanted to achieve, preserve, and avoid, he would be surprised by what he learned about himself.

After several minutes, he produced this list:

Achieve
   Steady, adequate income
   Opportunity to advance
   Variety of experience
   Proximity to work
   Stimulating work
   Budget management responsibility
   Entrepreneurial position
   Increased responsibility
   Professional growth
   Opportunity to be with family
   Springboard for next job
   Pride in work

Preserve
   Happy home life
   Self-confidence
   Continued residence in house for at least one more year

Avoid
   Likelihood that job doesn't work out

Next I asked him to rank each item on a rough scale (very high, high, medium, low). We looked over the list to see if there were any absolute requirements. What, for example, was an adequate income? To put it another way, what was the least he would accept? The first absolute requirement became $14,000 per year salary. "Any offer below that would rule out a job for consideration," he said, "no matter how attractive it is."

But I could see that Hugh was becoming impatient. "What's the sense of discussing a minimum salary of $14,000 when I already have two job offers for more than that?" he asked.

"I want to get down all your absolute requirements and see how the two jobs measure up," I replied. "You'll see the value in a few minutes."

He shrugged. Hugh listed as another absolute requirement "remaining in the same house for at least a year." He explained that leaving it now after all the time and energy they had invested in it would put a strain on their marriage.

Then he said something that puzzled me. "Another absolute requirement ought to be not working more than 40 hours a week, or at least the minimum number of hours over 40."

To me, the statement was a tipoff that Hugh had misstated the Purpose of his decision. I decided to test him to see if he could see the inconsistency.

"Why is it so important that you work a minimum of hours over 40?" I asked.

Hugh thought for a minute and said, "For two reasons: to have time to spend with my family and to have time to write music. You know how much enjoyment I get out of composing."

"But Hugh, I thought you wanted to make a statement or a mark or something through fund raising. Isn't that how you described your Purpose?"

"Well, yes, that's right."

"Do you really think you can make a mark if you're not going to be happy working more than 40 hours a week?" I said.

"Hey, man," he said, suddenly sitting bolt upright. "I'm not sure I want to make my mark as a fund raiser at all. I want to make my mark as a composer. That's what I want to do!"

"Then why are you considering these two job offers in fund raising?"

"I don't really know. What I really want to do, I guess, is to find a steady job that allows me to develop my earning power until I can support myself full time as a pop composer." Hugh broke into a smile from ear to ear. He had discovered what he really wanted to do with his life!

We proceeded to redefine his Purpose: "determine the best transition job that allows me to develop my earning power until I can write music full time." We then finished ranking his Criteria, measured the two Alternatives against them, and discovered that the college position was, by more than a 20 percent margin, the better opportunity. Chart O shows Hugh's analysis.

The key to choosing the college had been his statement of Purpose. Hugh had been leaning toward the position at the museum. It offered greater responsibility and would be a better springboard for his career as a fund raiser. But greater responsibility entailed longer hours. The position as director of development would have involved him in

**Chart O    Purpose: Find steady employment that allows me to develop my earning power until I can write music full time**

V = value
R = rating

| CRITERIA | ALTERNATIVE A College | | | ALTERNATIVE B Museum | | |
|---|---|---|---|---|---|---|
| **Absolute Requirements** | | | | | | |
| $14,000 per year minimum | Yes | | | Yes | | |
| Live in present home for at least one more year | Yes | | | Yes | | |
| **V        Desirable Objectives** | | R | V × R | | R | V × R |
| 10   Steady income | Very likely | 10 | 100 | Questionable financial status | 3 | 30 |
| 10   Happy home life | Forsee no problems | 10 | 100 | Some weekend work; evening meetings might interfere | 5 | 50 |
| 9   Minimum hours over 40 per week | 40 to 45 hours maximum | 10 | 90 | Could run to 50 or more hours | 5 | 45 |
| 8   Minimum likelihood that job won't work out | Don't see a problem | 10 | 80 | Some chance of problem but probably not | 7 | 56 |
| 7   Stimulating work | Quite stimulating | 7 | 49 | Very stimulating | 10 | 70 |
| 6   Maximum salary | $16,000 | 7 | 42 | $18,000 | 10 | 60 |
| 4   Springboard for next job | Very good chance; many small colleges | 8 | 32 | More demand for people who can shoulder responsibility | 10 | 40 |
| 3   Opportunity to grow professionally | Some | 6 | 18 | A lot | 10 | 30 |
| **TOTAL POINTS** | THE WINNER | | 546 | | | 431 |

evening and weekend fund-raising activities, for a total of 50 or more hours each week. Added to this burden was the uncertain financial status of the museum, which called into question his job security.

Hugh was buoyant that evening. While we feasted on lasagna, he treated us to his full repertoire of limericks. He had us doubled up with laughter.

As I prepared to leave, Joanne told me her husband hadn't been in such a good mood for months. Hugh thanked me for coming as I stepped into a cab. Then, almost as an afterthought, he added cheerfully: "Oh, by the way, thanks for helping me make up my mind too."

Eight months later I contacted Hugh at the college alumni office. He had received a raise after only six months on the job. He liked his work and was particularly pleased that the job left him free evenings and weekends to compose. Both he and Joanne believe Hugh made the right choice. It's worth noting, however, that he made the right choice only because the Seven Building Blocks forced him to face up to and reconcile the inconsistencies in his thinking.

If you are wrestling with the problem of choosing a career or taking a new job, the Building Blocks can guide you in your choice. Be sure you state your true Purpose and accurately weigh all your Criteria to reflect your true feelings, values, and judgments. Only then should you begin exploring possible jobs. The better you analyze your needs and wants, the more likely you are to find the job or career for you.

# 18

# The Housewife Who Went
# Back to Work

You're a housewife, 40 years old. Money is tight. Your oldest children are approaching college age. You haven't worked in almost 20 years. You're beginning to feel restless and unfulfilled at home. You want to go back to work. You're frightened and confused. Sure the want ads are clogged with job offers, but you don't know what you want to do or what you're qualified to do. Your husband is wary. He doesn't want you to take a job. He says there's no need for you to work, but you suspect the real reason for his reticence is pride. He'll feel he's let you down if he can't support the family on what he earns.

What do you do?

This is precisely the situation a neighbor of mine, Ellen, faced recently. We'll examine, step by step, how she resolved her problem. Then we'll demonstrate how you—or someone you know—can determine whether to go back to work and, if so, what kind of job to seek.

In resolving her problem, Ellen had the benefit of an understanding husband. He served as a sounding board in helping her sort out her feelings, establish her Priorities, and evaluate job Alternatives. But a friend or relative can do the job equally well. All it takes is the determination to control your future and a knowledge of the Seven Building Blocks.

When Ellen first discussed going back to work with her husband, Dan insisted it wasn't necessary. The next time she broached the subject, she tried a different tack. She stressed the benefits to her own well-being of "getting out into the real world, instead of just staring at the four walls all day."

Dan accepted that line of reasoning but suggested that it might be easier on Ellen to find a job working at home. "There are plenty of wives who do typing at home," he said, recalling that before their first child was born Ellen had spent several years as a secretary in a large stationery supply office.

"What do you think I could earn typing at home?" asked Ellen.

"Oh, I would say $125 a week," Dan replied.

Ellen said nothing. What she really wanted was to get out of the house and earn enough money—well over $125 a week—to help send the two oldest children to college.

What she calls her "great breakthrough" occurred several weeks later when she and Dan were engaged in that monthly American ritual known as trying to balance the checkbook. Observing the small gap between his income and the family's expenses, Dan confessed: "Of course we can all live on what I make"—"Of course," Ellen echoed quickly—"but paying those college tuitions is really going to be a problem if we don't get some more income."

"I could get a job," Ellen suggested. "But it doesn't seem to me that $125 a week, which is all I could earn typing at home, would be enough to pay for the kids' education."

"Well I guess we're going to have to do something," Dan said. "I'm not anxious for you to work, as you know. How do you really feel about taking a job, at least for a while? Would you mind?"

"Mind! I've been dying to go back to work. I think I'd be easier to live with if I had some feeling of accomplishment, if I felt I was doing something useful and getting paid for it."

But what kind of job? Ellen had enjoyed secretarial work and had kept up her skills by doing volunteer work for her church and a local hospital. She also had a knack for interior decorating and had made the couple's split-level home sparkle with color and imagination.

The next day Ellen called Janice, an old friend and a well-established interior decorator in the area. Janice invited her to her office showroom. Ellen returned in high spirits and announced to Dan that she was going to become an interior decorator. Janice had given her several leads for jobs and said she would happily serve as a reference.

Dan was heartened by Ellen's enthusiasm. But to spare her any possible disappointment, he suggested she also think about other kinds of jobs; he ticked off a list of friends and acquaintances who might be good leads for pursuing other opportunities. Ellen checked with a former neighbor who, on her own and with no previous experience, had started a jewelry firm and was always looking for saleswomen. She also had an enjoyable phone chat with a college roommate who now ran a boutique and who said she might have a position in sales or modeling if Ellen had retained her schoolgirl figure (she had indeed).

Ellen touched bases with two doctors she knew from church who she thought might be looking for a typist, receptionist, or file clerk. Both were encouraging. They had no openings at the moment but were willing to check with friends if she was really interested. And her brother, a buyer for a chain of department stores, said he knew of an opening for a receptionist.

With all these possibilities confusing Ellen, Dan suggested she call me. He had participated in a project team I headed to help his company accelerate the introduction of a new minicomputer system. "The system helped us find the best way of doing what we wanted to do; it may be able to help you find the best way of doing what you want to do," he told Ellen.

Ellen was reluctant. In addition to having an aversion to making lists, she thought that probing her thoughts and feelings would be too time-consuming and too exhausting. To please Dan, however she relented and called me.


To her surprise, I agreed that making up your mind can be difficult. "The hard thing about the process is not the lists or the weights. The hard thing is being really honest with yourself," I told her when we met in my office a few days later. "You have to determine what you truly want to achieve, not just what you think would please others. You must do your best to separate the few objectives that you *absolutely have to meet* from those that look important but in actuality are not. Comparing one objective against another and deciding which is more important—and how much more important it is—can wear you out."

Ellen said she appreciated my frankness but added, "I'm not sure it's worth going through all that."

"Which makes more sense, Ellen? To spend some time thinking through these things before you select a job, or to risk being terribly disappointed afterward?"

She sighed. "You're right, I guess."


Because Ellen was so anxious, I suggested that she not make a decision immediately. I told her to think through her options over the next few days. Dan could serve as a sounding board and doublecheck the information she obtained on each of the jobs that interested her.

"The day the worksheets arrived in the mail," Ellen told me later, "Dan and I got down to work. It wasn't hard to get through Building Block No. 1, smoking out the Issues. Why was a decision necessary? Because I wanted to earn as much as possible for the children's education. Nor did we have any trouble with Building Block No. 2, stating my Purpose. The answer was to determine the best type of work for me. Then came Building Block No. 3, setting my Criteria. We thought about what I wanted to acheive, preserve, and avoid. We really went whole hog on this, ending up with a list of two dozen Criteria."

Here is Ellen's list:

## PURPOSE

Determine the best type of work for me

## CRITERIA

Achieve
  The most money
  Lowest mileage to and from work (gas expense)
  Meeting interesting people
  Feeling of accomplishment
  Pleasant work atmosphere
  Comfortable amount of work
  Office privacy
  Freedom to work independently
  Good level of responsibility
  Appreciation and recognition for my work
  Learning new area of work (broadening myself)
  Working for a person with intelligence and understanding
  Normal working hours (8:00 to 5:30)

Preserve
  Family responsibilities
  Friendships
  Hobbies (golf, tennis, art)

Avoid
  Working with "catty" people
  Large office
  High-pressure job
  Large volume of typing
  Having someone constantly on my back
  Menial tasks
  Dull work
  More than a 40-hour week

"Building Block No. 4, establishing my Priorities, was tough to do."

Ellen continued. "Dan and I went through the Criteria, eliminating duplications and grouping the items. For example, we took 'good level of responsibility' and 'comfortable amount of work' and placed them under 'feeling of accomplishment.' We also revised some of the Criteria. We changed 'avoiding more than a 40-hour week' to 'weekend work rare'; added the Criterion of 'taking occasional time off when needed'; mixed in 'normal working hours'; and put all of these under 'preserving family responsibilities.'

"But ranking was a problem. First I insisted there were at least ten absolute requirements. Then I pared the list down to three: earning a minimum of $175 per week; driving a maximum of ten miles each way from work; and not leaving the house before 8:00 A.M. and getting home by 6:00 P.M.

"I ruled out the other seven as absolute requirements because they didn't meet these two tests":

1.   Is the Criterion so important that any Solution *absolutely has to* satisfy it to be acceptable?
2.   If so, how do you know (i.e., is it measurable)?

"Down the drain on the measure test went 'freedom to work independently'—neither Dan nor I could figure out how we could test Alternatives on that standard. Dan also pointed out that he and the kids could help out at home more, depending on my workload, thus giving me less responsibility to shoulder. So 'preserving family responsibilities,' which I had also thought of as an absolute requirement, became just 'highly desirable.'

"After separating out the absolute requirements, Dan and I went to work ranking the desirable objectives—establishing the most important one, the second most important, and so forth. I had a lot of trouble figuring out the order of importance, but Dan's questions helped me understand how I felt about each one. He kept asking, 'If you had to drop one of these, which would you drop? Why?'"

These are the Priorities that Ellen set:

**PURPOSE**
Determine the best type of work for me

**CRITERIA**
What I want to achieve, preserve, and avoid as problems (grouped and ranked in order, from most important to least important):

Relative Ranking

*Maximum earnings**                                    1
   With added pay for overtime
   Possibility of bonus or profit sharing, etc.

*Freedom to work independently**                       2
   Without high pressure
   Without anybody on my back
   With some office privacy
   Avoid large office environment

*Feeling of accomplishment**                           3
   Responsible position
   Avoid dull work (like large typing load)
   Avoid menial jobs (like coffee servant for men)
   Comfortable amount of work

*Time for family responsibilities**                    4
   Normal working hours*
   Weekend work rare
   Occasional time off when needed

*Pleasant work atmosphere**                            5
   Meet interesting people*
   Avoid obnoxious or "catty" people

*Appreciation and recognition of my work**             6
   Work for intelligent, understanding person*

*Time for friends*                                     7
   Be able to meet them for lunch

*Time for hobbies (golf, tennis, art)*                 8

*Personal growth*                                      9
   Learn new kind of work

Next Ellen assigned values to the objectives, as follows:

## PURPOSE

Determine the best type of work for me

## CRITERIA

   Absolute Requirements
      Minimum of $175 per week
      Maximum of ten miles each way from work of nonreimbursable expense
      Not leave house before 8:00 A.M. and home ordinarily by 6:00 P.M.·

---

*Originally thought of as absolute requirements.

Desirable Objectives

10 *Maximum earnings*
    With added pay for overtime
    Possibility of bonus, profit sharing, and other benefits

8 *Freedom to work independently*
    Without high pressure
    Without anybody on my back
    With some office privacy
    Avoid large office environment

7 *Feeling of accomplishment*
    Responsible position
    Avoid dull work (like large typing load)
    Avoid menial jobs (like coffee servant for men)
    Comfortable amount of work

5 *Time for family responsibilities*
    Normal working hours
    Weekend work rare
    Occasional time off when needed

4 *Pleasant work atmosphere*
    Meet interesting people
    Avoid obnoxious or "catty" people

3 *Appreciation and recognition of my work*
    Work for intelligent, understanding person

2 *Time for friends*
    Be able to meet them for lunch

1 *Time for hobbies (golf, tennis, art)*

1 *Personal growth*
    Learn new kind of work

"After my Priorities were set," Ellen continued, "I began Building Block No. 5, the search for Solutions. Here I abbreviated the process. I'm sure there are hundreds of jobs that I could have considered. But I felt I'd be happy with the choices we had already come up with, so I drew a matrix with the Criteria down the left side and a list of possible Solutions across the top. In the blocks I wrote down what we knew about each job and evaluated how well it did against each Criterion. The results began to show almost immediately.

"The possible choices were receptionist, interior decorator, boutique model and saleswoman, doctor's assistant, secretary, and jewelry manufacturer's representative. I eliminated the job as receptionist because my research showed it would not meet my absolute requirement of earning at least $175 a week. 'Maximum earnings,' a 10-weighted objective, was probably best achieved if I became an interior decorator, so I gave it a score of 10. Manufacturer's rep was a close second. I rated it an 8. Secretarial work was lower but had some earning power, so I gave it a 6. Boutique work, which was barely above minimum, got only a 1. Work in a doctor's office would pay only the minimum requirement of $175 (at least to start), so it got a 0.

"I wasn't sure of all the answers by a long shot. But I put down the best information Dan and I could find and sprinkled in a number of question marks, which I removed as we did more research. When I finally fit in all the information I needed, I scored the Alternatives and compared the totals. "The winner was interior decorating; just what I thought I wanted!

"But, for some reason I didn't understand, I felt uneasy. And the instructions I had told me why. Looking at the information, I saw that even though interior decorating had the best overall score, it was only 8 points ahead of secretarial work, a difference of only 2 percent. Interior decorating did the best job on 'maximum earnings' (which I had weighted 10), and it did as good a job as any of the Alternatives on giving me a 'feeling of accomplishment' (which I had weighted 7). But it did next to the poorest job on 'freedom to work independently' (which I had weighted 8).

"To me, working independently meant—as I had written on the chart—working without high pressure and without anybody on my back. I remembered hearing my interior decorator friend complain about how difficult it was to get delivery on certain colors and fabrics and how impatient customers became with delays, no matter how justified they were. Though I like to think I can take criticism, in fact I'm very sensitive. I frankly don't think I can handle continual complaints without becoming frustrated or severely discouraged."

Ellen's analysis is shown in Chart P. What conclusions would you draw about the best choice of a career for her?

"Dan and I both studied the chart and rechecked my arithmetic," Ellen continued. "I found myself getting increasingly frustrated. 'What is it telling me?' I asked Dan. 'Is interior decorating the best choice for me or not?'

"'Honey,' Dan replied, 'what this chart says to me is that interior decorating is a slightly better choice. But if you're concerned about having people on your back and being under pressure, maybe it's not for you.'"

Since there was not at least a 15 percent difference between Alternatives B and E and since both Alternatives had drawbacks on highly

## CHART P    Purpose:

V = value
R = rating

| CRITERIA | ALTERNATIVE A | ALTERNATIVE B | | | ALTERNATIVE C | | |
|---|---|---|---|---|---|---|---|
| | Receptionist | Interior Decorator | | | Boutique Saleswoman | | |
| **Absolute Requirements** | | | | | | | |
| Minimum of $175 per week | No ($150) | Yes, 30% commission ($175 to $400) | | | Yes ($185) | | |
| Maximum of 10 miles each way from work of nonreimbursable expense | | 80% travel, reimbursed | | | Up to 5 miles | | |
| Not leave house before 8:00 A.M. and home ordinarily by 6:00 P.M. | | Set own hours | | | 10:00 to 5:30 | | |
| V   Desirable Objectives | | | R | V × R | | R | V × R |
| 10   Maximum earnings | | 30% commission ($175 to $400) | 10 | 100 | $185 plus $25; more? | 3 | 30 |
| 8   Freedom to work independently | | Definitely yes | 7 | 56 | Moderate | 8 | 64 |
| 7   Feeling of accomplishment | | Very good with some frustration | 10 | 70 | Excellent | 9 | 63 |
| 5   Time for family responsibilities | | Should be able to, but evenings and Saturdays could interfere | 3 | 15 | Pretty good except for Saturday work | 6 | 30 |
| 4   Pleasant work atmosphere | | Should be excellent except for some people! | 10 | 40 | Should be excellent except for some people | 7 | 28 |
| 3   Appreciation and recognition of my work | | Satisfied customers; recognition from owner too! | 10 | 30 | Sales slip tells it all! | 8 | 24 |
| 2   Time for friends | | I can pretty much set my own hours | 10 | 20 | Very good | 9 | 18 |
| 1   Time for hobbies (golf, tennis, art) | | Flexible hours | 10 | 10 | Little time | 2 | 2 |
| 1   Personal growth | | Excellent | 10 | 10 | Very good | 8 | 8 |
| TOTAL POINTS | | THE WINNER? | | 351 | | | 267 |

# Determine the best type of work for me

| ALTERNATIVE D<br><br>Doctor's Assistant | | | ALTERNATIVE E<br><br>Secretary | | | ALTERNATIVE F<br>Jewelry Manufacturer's<br>Representative | | |
|---|---|---|---|---|---|---|---|---|
| Yes ($175)<br><br>Up to 10 miles<br><br><br>9:00 to 5:30 | | | Yes ($175 to $230)<br><br>Up to 10 miles<br><br><br>8:30 or 9:00 to 5:30 | | | Yes, 20% commisssion<br>($175 to $325)<br>100% travel, reimbursed<br><br><br>Set own hours | | |
| | R | V × R | | R | V × R | | R | V × R |
| $175 tops | 0 | 0 | $175 to $250 plus Christmas bonus | 6 | 60 | 20% commission ($175 to $325) | 8 | 80 |
| Moderate | 8 | 64 | Only take job that's "very good" | 10 | 80 | Definitely yes | 5 | 40 |
| Not much | 3 | 21 | Excellent with careful selection | 10 | 70 | Good but some frustration | 8 | 56 |
| Shouldn't be too much of a problem | 8 | 40 | Seems to be best one; won't take job requiring overtime | 10 | 50 | Pretty good | 7 | 35 |
| Good or very good | 6 | 24 | Should be excellent | 10 | 40 | Only fair | 4 | 16 |
| Probably not much; just expected | 3 | 9 | Boss will make the difference; check this in interview | 6 | 18 | Up to me to pat myself on the back | 6 | 18 |
| Regimented, so it may be difficult | 5 | 10 | Only little better than doctor's office | 6 | 12 | Set my own hours | 10 | 20 |
| Little time | 2 | 2 | Little time | 2 | 2 | Flexible hours | 10 | 10 |
| Not really | 1 | 1 | Possibly | 5 | 5 | Fair | 3 | 3 |
| | | 171 | THE WINNER? | | 337 | | | 278 |

rated Criteria (B on "freedom to work independently," E on "maximum earnings"), Ellen went back to the drawing board. She needed to clarify her own values and explore how to overcome the shortcomings of one or more of the Alternatives.

"I was beginning to understand the whole business," said Ellen, "and I suddenly felt relieved. At Dan's suggestion, I talked with Janice to see if my judgments about interior decorating were accurate. She still encouraged me to get into the field, but she conceded, 'You're at the mercy of suppliers who sometimes cancel colors or oversell items, and you often find yourself unable to get the material customers want.'

"I wrote off interior decorating and began to look at the strengths and weaknesses of secretarial work. As I reviewed the chart, I found that it rated very well on every important Criterion except one—'maximum earnings.' I had scored it only a 6 on that Criterion because being a secretary generally pays less than being a decorator or a jewelry manufacturer's rep. On the other hand, maybe I could find a job at a starting salary higher than $175 a week, with a raise after two or three months if my performance were really good. And if there were a Christmas bonus, maybe I was being too pessimistic in scoring secretarial work only a 6 on 'maximum earnings.'

"Since secretarial work looked better to me than interior decorating, had no significant negatives, and rated 18 percent higher than the next two choices—jewelry manufacturer's rep and boutique saleswoman—it seemed to be the best choice. The remaining alternative—doctor's assistant—scored so far behind that it wasn't worth investigating. Dan agreed with my analysis and I set about looking into different secretarial jobs."

Using her own and her husband's contacts, Ellen talked with executives, secretaries, and typists in a variety of offices to learn of their experiences and advice. What was the boss like? How intelligent and understanding was he? What kind of pressures were involved in the job? How much responsibility and freedom was there? Ellen discovered that she could use her absolute requirements and desirable objectives as questions to raise in her job interviews.

Three weeks after deciding to seek secretarial work, Ellen found a job in a large advertising agency. She got a raise after only a month and a second raise five months later. "I'm working for a woman, which I find very refreshing and totally unexpected," she told me later. "My boss is intelligent and considerate; she's giving me more and more responsibility, letting me decide things for myself and carry them through to the end. When she gave me the two raises within six months, she said it was because I was able to handle work that she had always had to do for herself."

After almost 20 years as a homemaker, Ellen found a satisfying job on her first try. She didn't spend weeks chasing down leads in different fields on the chance that one of them might suit her. She determined the kind of job she wanted in a few evenings at home with the help of her "sounding board" husband. He helped draw out her real objectives and sort out the Criteria she felt strongly about from those she only *thought* she felt strongly about.

By the time Ellen began looking for a job, she knew just what she wanted—not only the kind of work but the atmosphere she wanted to work in and the pitfalls and rewards. The Criteria did it, the Priorities did it, the matrix did it, the evaluation did it. When she finished the process, she had a confidence in her decision that often eludes job seekers who don't systematically analyze their objectives.

Choosing the best job requires careful analysis. By doing some hard thinking, you can identify your true feelings and turn your emotions into a positive force for change.

# 19

# Changing Careers in Midlife

All of us who work for a living have probably thought at one time or another of finding a new career. But few of us do anything about it. According to the U.S. Bureau of Labor Statistics, 15.5 million Americans quit or changed jobs in 1976, yet only an estimated 1 million changed occupations.

Is the reason lack of desire? Apparently not. In a survey of middle managers conducted in 1973, the American Management Associations found that 70 percent expected to explore a change of careers in the foreseeable future. Public opinion surveys generally find that a majority of workers are unhappy with their jobs. What keeps them from leaving? There are a host of reasons, including security, inertia, fear of the unknown, and a belief that the alternatives are less attractive. The expressions of work frustration have become commonplace:

"It's just a job."
"It puts food on the table."
"Sorry, I just work here."
"There must be an easier way to earn a living."

Few people ever sit down and plan their work lives, asking themselves, "What is my purpose in choosing a career? What do I want to achieve, preserve, and avoid by any career choice? What are the various ways of satisfying these objectives? Which appears most promising? What do I have to do to qualify for the career choice that seems most attractive? What could go wrong with the choice I have made?"

When we're young, it seldom occurs to us to plan our work lives. When we're middle-aged, we think it's too late. Well, it's never too late—though, let's face it, it can be more difficult as we get older. If we're unhappy with what we're doing, or if our job seems to be leading to a dead end, it makes sense at least to consider a change of careers. In today's work world technology is rendering more and more skills obsolete while medical science is prolonging our productive years. As a result, there may be a career change in our future whether we plan for it or not.

My good friends Jack and Bonnie Clements did more than change jobs. They did more than change careers. They transformed their lives. A discussion of moving closer to Jack's high-paying but unchallenging job in New York City gave birth to a carefully thought-out plan that eventually set them down on an island in the Caribbean, where they found lesser-paying but more meaningful work.

Their story is a model of the careful use of the Building Block techniques. By studying Jack and Bonnie's situation you can learn how to use the Building Blocks to change your career and perhaps your life.

Jack was the $60,000-a-year personnel director for an international manufacturer of plumbing fixtures. Bonnie, a nurse by training, had been out of the job market for ten years but was thinking of looking for a job once again. The couple were in their late forties. Both had been married and divorced previously. Between them they had three children, a 19-year-old boy in college and two others bound for college soon: a boy of 17 and a girl of 15.

After their marriage four years earlier, Jack and Bonnie had bought a comfortable frame colonial house in the Connecticut suburbs of New York City. It was a long commute to the office for Jack—an hour and a half each way by train—but the location enabled him to be near his father, who had terminal cancer. After the elder Mr. Clements died, Bonnie began to think about selling the house and moving closer to Jack's work.

She brought up the subject one rainy Sunday while she and Jack were relaxing with the newspaper after a leisurely breakfast. "I've been thinking about your commuting, Jack, and how much it takes out of you, spending three hours on a train day in and day out. Maybe it's time we sold the house and bought something closer to your job."

Jack put down his paper and pursed his lips. "That's an idea," he said. "Let's think about it. I sure wouldn't mind getting home a little earlier and spending more time together."

But the more Jack thought about the idea, the less he liked it. He'd developed a habit of skimming the job ads each weekend—"more out of curiosity than anything else," he told himself. Now he began to wonder if his motives weren't more than curiosity. After dinner a few days later he shared his misgivings with Bonnie.

"Remember the idea you had of moving closer to my job?"

"Sure."

"Well, I don't know if I like it."

Bonnie seemed taken aback. "Then you really don't mind the commuting?"

"I do mind it, but I think we may be barking up the wrong tree. Instead of thinking of a new house, maybe we should be thinking of a new job." He explained that for some time he had had the "gnawing feeling" that things could be better. "I'm not sure what the problem is, but somehow I don't get much satisfaction out of what I'm doing."

To his surprise, Bonnie said she had sensed that he was becoming restless at work. "What is it about the job you don't like?"

"I don't know. I can't put my finger on it. I just don't find it, well, fulfilling."

For the next week Jack kept asking himself, "What's wrong with my job?" He could find no satisfactory answer. On the contrary, he could find a lot of reasons to be satisfied: it was the best-paying job he had ever had; it offered responsibility, normal working hours, a pleasant working environment, friendly colleagues, good job security, and excellent fringe and retirement benefits.

Unable to identify the source of his dissatisfaction, Jack sat down with Bonnie the following weekend for an exercise in "turning the coin over." "Even if we can't immediately pinpoint why you're unhappy at work," said Bonnie, "maybe we can figure out what kind of work would make you happy, which is another way of attacking the same problem."

Both Jack and Bonnie had received extensive training in the use of the Building Blocks. In less than a minute they were able to smoke out the Issues and state their Purpose (Building Blocks Nos. 1 and 2). Why was a decision necessary? "Because I'm dissatisfied with my job." What did they need to determine? "The best kind of job for Jack."

Setting Criteria (Building Block No. 3) didn't appear to be a problem either. One important Criterion, they decided, was to live closer to work. Another was to have a bigger salary and better compensation package. Jack thought the bigger salary would come in handy in sending the two younger kids to college. Bonnie suggested, jokingly, that the bigger compensation package would be helpful "in case you kick off."

Jack wasn't amused. He poured martinis for himself and Bonnie and sat down. "You know, it may sound corny, but I want to do something rewarding, something where you can see that people are better off for your involvement. In the last 24 years, ever since I started working for big corporations, I can think of only two or three times that people were better off because of what I did. And I'm in personnel work! That's sad."

Jack took a sip of his cocktail, then continued. "Another thing, you know I'd really love to do something tangible. I'm tired of the never-never land of people and organizations and paper pushing. I want to do something I can really get my hands into."

Bonnie mulled that over. "Are you talking about a change of jobs or a change of careers?"

"I don't know exactly. I've always enjoyed leading seminars. Maybe I'd like teaching."

"Wait a minute," cried Bonnie. "We're not ready to talk about Solutions yet. We're still deciding what you'd like in a job."

They spent about an hour compiling a list of Criteria. Over the next few days, when each of them thought of another Criterion that any change in jobs or careers should meet, they jotted it down and then discussed it, deciding whether to include it or not.

Some of Jack's objectives were hard to boil down into a few words. For example, he said he wanted "to be able to throw a switch and see a light." He recalled how, as a child, he enjoyed helping his carpenter father fix up homes in the Midwest. "It would be so good to smell fresh-cut lumber as I put up a house, or run my hands along cold copper tubing, or hear the sound of a piece of equipment starting up. Maybe I sound crazy, but I really like the idea of getting into something like that."

They defined that Criterion as "working with hands" but later changed it to "using mechanical ability."

If Jack became a carpenter or another kind of tradesman, he would have to take a severe cut in pay—at a time when they would need extra money for the two younger children headed for college. Bonnie volunteered to go back to work. "I've really been looking for an excuse to find a nursing job. If it will help you to do what you really want to do, we'll both be happier for it," she explained.

As they probed deeper into the possibilities of making a major change in their lives, it became clear that out of Jack's original "gnawing feeling" and Bonnie's concern for his commuting a new life plan was evolving. "The amazing thing," Bonnie told me later, "is that we began to understand ourselves and each other better than we ever had before. The approach became the vehicle for communication, a lifeline between us. We began to understand what we really wanted out of life."

The couple posted their list of Criteria—the things they wanted to achieve, preserve, and avoid—on the refrigerator door. Over the next few weeks, they made changes and put rough Priorities (Building Block No. 4) on the Criteria. Either of them could make changes, but the rule was that the reason for any change had to be discussed.

They also focused their search for Solutions (Building Block No. 5) on the refrigerator door, which they began referring to as the Oracle. (Bonnie would say, "I see from the Oracle that you're considering a couple of new careers. Is that right?" They would both laugh.)

It was during this period that the Purpose of their decision underwent a subtle but significant change. No longer was their Purpose to "determine the best job for Jack"; instead, they decided it should be to "determine the best place to live and the best type of work for us." At one point they had this list, with their tentative Criteria ranked on a rough scale of very high (VH) or high (H):

## PURPOSE
Determine the best place to live and the best type of work for us

## TENTATIVE CRITERIA
Absolute Requirements
    Rewarding career—make contribution (Jack)
    Job in medicine (Bonnie)
    Best location to balance job and family
    Opportunity to use mechanical ability (Jack)
    Close relationship with children
    Accessibility of children to our former spouses
    Minimum upset to children

Desirable Objectives
    VH  Maximum income
    VH  Increased benefits
    VH  Maximum time together
    VH  Teaching activity or relationship
    VH  Contact with friends and relatives
     H  Minimum commuting time
     H  Low monthly home expenses

## POSSIBLE SOLUTIONS—JOBS

For Jack
Carpenter
Electrician
Mason
Teacher (psychology, industrial arts, business administration)
Vocational guidance counselor
Two of the above

For Bonnie
Nurse (hospital, clinic, home health, doctor's office)
Medical laboratory
Teacher of nursing
Nursing administrator

## POSSIBLE SOLUTIONS—PLACES

??????

Jack and Bonnie frequently found themselves rejuggling their Priorities. "Minimum commuting," which had originally been Bonnie's most important Criterion, became considerably less as time went on. She reasoned that it was more important to be happy in what they were doing than to minimize commuting. Similarly, "maximum income" and "increased benefits," which had been rated "very high" were downgraded to "medium" Priorities.

The couple decided they would not make any changes until Bonnie's daughter turned 18. That gave them three years to plan. "I had always been concerned with making more money," Jack told me. "But now I found myself asking, 'What for?' Finding rewarding work became more important."

College expenses were a concern, of course, but the kids had always planned to work to help with their expenses. As Jack explained it: "We reasoned that with our two incomes plus what we could save from my salary in the three years, we would be able to make ends meet. The house in Connecticut was costing us a fortune in mortgage payments, taxes, and heating oil. Without that burden, our costs would be a lot less."

As Jack and Bonnie analyzed their situation, they faced two independent but related questions: What should they do? Where should they do it?

The "where" turned out to be a bit more sticky than the "what." The children wanted to stay in the New York City area, and at first Bonnie felt that the couple should remain near them. But after a family conference on the problem, it was decided that if Jack and Bonnie were no more than five hours away by plane, the children could have the independence they wanted and still maintain the security they might need.

"Suddenly," Jack said later, "we felt that we had embarked on a great adventure, with the whole world at our feet."

Of course, having to be no more than five hours away by plane did rule out some locations, such as the northern coast of the Mediterranean and the Greek islands, both of which Jack had become enchanted with on vacation before meeting Bonnie. On the other hand, five hours by air from New York City meant that they could live in any number of places: Florida, Canada, Mexico, the Virgin Islands, or the Caribbean.

Still, they had to proceed carefully. They needed information about all the places that interested them. How much did it cost to live there? Could Jack work as a mechanic and perhaps teach? Could Bonnie work in a medical laboratory or a hospital? What were the people like? How hard would it be to adjust? As they listed their questions, they understood the enormity of the change they were contemplating.

I met Jack for lunch on a business trip during this period. He told me their plans and said that he and Bonnie had collected information about possible locations from travel agencies, libraries, real estate brokers, and consulates. They were also planning some trips. The information helped refine their Criteria and simplify their selection. For example, because they both loved warm weather and sandy beaches, they made that one of their absolute requirements.

The refrigerator door became so cluttered with notes that they copied the information about possible locations and types of work into a notebook, which they promptly dubbed Oracle II. In total, they considered at one point or another eight locations: the northern coast of the Mediterranean, the Greek Islands, southern Florida, the U.S. Virgin Islands, the British Virgin Islands, Guadaloupe-Martinique, Granada, and the coast of Mexico.

The information they collected about Florida suggested that Jack would have trouble finding work there. The Florida construction industry had a surplus of experienced tradesmen, and Jack, as a novice, could hardly compete.

They researched several islands in the Caribbean, ruling out those that were noted for political instability or locations more than five hours by air from New York.

Both Jack and Bonnie had traveled abroad and were enthusiastic about the prospect of living in a foreign environment. But they wanted to retain some contact with people of similar backgrounds to theirs. Jack had spent a year in London in the 1950s and had a special fondness for things British. That, plus its beaches and sand, made the British Virgin Islands particularly attractive.

As soon as they could, they set out for an inspection tour of the British Virgin Islands. To his great satisfaction, Jack found that several of the islands needed electricians to install and service refrigeration and air-conditioning equipment. He inquired about the requirements for the job and returned with a list of courses he would need in order to qualify. Shortly after returning from the islands, Jack checked with a service contractor and learned that a local college offered courses in air-conditioning and refrigeration services. He inquired about enrolling.

Jack and Bonnie then completed their matrix and tested the Alternatives (Building Block No. 6). Their analysis is shown in Chart Q. The winner, by a margin of 17 percent, was the British Virgin Islands.

They carefully troubleshot their decision (Building Block No. 7) to see what problems the move would involve. Would Jack be able to take his company profit-sharing plan with him? Could he convert his company medical and life insurance policies into private policies? How would they cope with a possible family crisis? How often could they arrange to talk to the children by phone and visit with them, either on the islands or in the States? What if the job didn't work out? What if they became homesick? They made plans to cope with these eventualities and carefully planned their move.

As it turned out, Jack's travel schedule prevented him from taking the college course. But the service contractor suggested a correspondence school with a national reputation. The contractor's nephew had taken courses there and obtained a well-paying job afterward.

Jack enrolled in the school. His studies proceeded slowly because of his workload and his desire to spend as much time as possible with the family. After almost two years he completed the course and began to service his own and some friends' equipment. Lo and behold, the appliances invariably ran better after he worked on them.

He and Bonnie visited the British Virgin Islands three more times. Bonnie was promised 20 hours' work a week as a nurse in a hospital. The builder of a large resort assured Jack of a job as an electrican and air-conditioning mechanic. Jack applied for a job teaching psychology and business administration in an adult education program. On their last trip Jack and Bonnie put a downpayment on a small home near the beach.

When Jack and Bonnie moved to the British Virgin Islands, his younger son was a college junior and her daughter had successfully completed her first semester at a state university. More than a year passed before I heard from them. Jack sent me a postcard saying he was

V = value
R = rating

**CHART Q     Purpose:**

| CRITERIA | ALTERNATIVE A<br>Northern coast of Mediterranean | ALTERNATIVE B<br>Greek Islands | ALTERNATIVE C<br>Southern Florida | ALTERNATIVE D<br>U.S. Virgin Islands | | |
|---|---|---|---|---|---|---|
| **Absolute Requirements** | | | | | | |
| No more than 5 hours by air from New York City | No | No | Yes | Yes (3½ hours) | | |
| Year-round climate of 75° to 85° with sand and beaches | | | Yes | Yes | | |
| Stable political and social environment | | | Yes. | Unsettled; questionable | | |
| Opportunity for social contact with people of background similar to ours | | | Yes | Yes | | |
| Steady employment opportunities for both of us in our chosen fields (electrical/refrigeration and nursing/laboratory work) | | | No | Yes | | |
| **V Desirable Objectives** | | | | | V | V × R |
| 10   Reasonable income commensurate with cost of living | | | | Yes | 10 | 100 |
| 10   Maximum feeling of achievement and impact | | | | Likely | 7 | 70 |
| 8   Opportunity to make personal social contribution | | | | Maybe | 5 | 40 |
| 8   Maximum time for ourselves | | | | Yes | 10 | 80 |
| 6   Moderate pace of life | | | | Yes | 10 | 60 |
| 6   Friendly people | | | | Yes, but unrest | 6 | 30 |
| 5   Opportunity to teach | | | | Probable but not certain | 7 | 35 |
| 4   No need to learn and be competent in a new language | | | | English spoken | 10 | 40 |
| 4   Culture contrast with U.S. without culture shock | | | | Same | 5 | 20 |
| 2   Within 5 hours by air of New York City | | | | 3½ hours | 10 | 20 |
| TOTAL POINTS | | | | | | 501 |

## Determine the best place to live and the best type of work for us

| ALTERNATIVE E | | | ALTERNATIVE F | ALTERNATIVE G | ALTERNATIVE H | | |
|---|---|---|---|---|---|---|---|
| British Virgin Islands | | | Guadeloupe–Martinique | Grenada | Coast of Mexico | | |
| Yes (3½ hours) | | | Yes (4½ hours) | No (6½ hours) | Yes (5 hours) | | |
| Yes | | | Yes | | Yes | | |
| Yes | | | Questionable | | Yes, but minor unrest | | |
| Yes, but limited | | | Very little | | Yes | | |
| Yes | | | No | | Marginal for aliens | | |
| | V | V × R | | | | V | V × R |
| Appears probable | 8 | 80 | | | Difficult | 2 | 20 |
| Yes | 10 | 100 | | | Probable | 8 | 80 |
| Yes | 10 | 80 | | | May be difficult | 3 | 24 |
| Yes | 10 | 80 | | | Yes | 10 | 80 |
| Yes | 10 | 60 | | | Yes | 10 | 60 |
| Yes | 10 | 60 | | | Mixed | 5 | 30 |
| Yes | 10 | 50 | | | Possibly | 4 | 20 |
| English spoken | 10 | 40 | | | Should learn Spanish | 4 | 16 |
| Excellent | 10 | 40 | | | Fair | 3 | 12 |
| 3½ hours | 10 | 20 | | | 5 hours | 0 | 0 |
| THE WINNER | | 610 | | | | | 342 |

going to be in New York to attend to some personal affairs. I arranged to meet him again for lunch. He showed up looking a good ten years younger—and several shades darker—than I remembered him.

"I feel like a new man. Life is an adventure down there. You can't believe how beautiful it is." He explained that he was working full time with his hands, keeping the islands cool by installing and servicing refrigeration equipment. "It sure beats spending three hours a day on a grimy train," he said. Bonnie was working as a nurse in the local hospital.

"It turns out there are some problems," he continued. "The slow pace of life drove us crazy at first. We're not used to waiting when we want something. I'm sure a lot of people there—and here too—think we're crazy to have done what we did. I haven't been able to find any way to teach, which is something I'm disappointed about. But I have been able to set up a part-time counseling service advising islanders how to turn their talents into rewarding jobs. Bonnie's daughter had difficulty adjusting to university life. You should have seen our phone bill the first few months!" But, turning the problem into an opportunity, the couple had the three children flown to the islands for the first Christmas. "I think our determination to control our own lives has helped the children see that they can make their own futures just as we have."

If you're dissatisfied with your life, the Building Blocks can help you clarify your goals and decide how best to reach them. The process helped Jack and Bonnie Clements to plan the life they wanted and to live it. Using these simple decision-making techniques, they stopped being "victims of circumstances" and forged their own future.

# 20

## What Are You Doing Today . . . Tomorrow . . . the Rest of Your Life?

If you have read this book carefully, you now have at your disposal something that money can't buy: a clear and systematic method for making effective decisions. What will you do with it?

You can make the system work for you, bringing to bear on the problems you want to resolve the full benefit of your experience, your knowledge, your insight, and your values. Or you can ignore the system and make decisions the way you always have. For most people, that means making decisions haphazardly and often by default.

How do you begin to use it? Think of some problem you face or have postponed facing. Someone whose feelings you have hurt, a phone call you have avoided making, a child whose behavior you want to deal with, an investment decision you want to make, someone you would like to do something special for. Then sit down *right now* to "work your issue." Give yourself, say, 20 minutes. No interruptions. Follow the Building Blocks step by step:

1. SMOKE OUT THE ISSUES: *Why is a decision necessary?*
2. STATE YOUR PURPOSE: *What needs to be determined?*
3. SET YOUR CRITERIA: *What are the objectives that any solution must achieve, preserve, and avoid?*

4. ESTABLISH YOUR PRIORITIES: *What criteria must a solution absolutely satisfy to be effective? What other criteria should it meet (ranked in order of importance)?*

5. SEARCH FOR SOLUTIONS: *What are the possible ways of meeting the criteria you've established?*

6. TEST THE ALTERNATIVES: *How does each alternative stack up against the priorities?*

7. TROUBLESHOOT YOUR DECISION: *What could go wrong with the alternative you've chosen? How can the decision be improved?*

Spend your 20 minutes working on any problem that confronts you: Should you pick up the kids at school or let them walk home? Should you board the dog when you go skiing for the weekend or ask a neighbor to take care of him? What should you buy your mother for her birthday? Should you fix the old lawnmower or buy a new one? These are what we called vanilla-or-chocolate decisions in Chapter 13—everyday decisions of no apparent lasting consequence. Resolve one such decision today. Then reserve 20 minutes tomorrow to work on another.

Gradually work up to bigger issues: Should you look for a new home? What should you do on vacation next year? Remember, you must ask yourself, "What do I want to achieve, preserve, and avoid by whatever I decide to do?" Then, "Which of these objectives are absolute requirements and which are desirable but not essential?" Only then should you ask, "What are the possible ways of satisfying these objectives? Which of these does the best job? How can it be altered to do an even better job of satisfying the objectives?"

Eventually, you will be proficient enough in using the Seven Building Blocks to tackle the big issues: What do you want from your friendships, your marriage, your relationship with your loved ones, your career? Finally, what do you want to do with your life?

Here's how one man used the Building Blocks to plan his future when, at the age of 57, he found himself out of a job for the first time in his life. Ken had built a successful manufacturing business after World War II. But he watched his profits plummet during the mid-1950s when foreign competitors with lower labor costs began copying his products and undercutting his prices. A firm believer in the work ethic, he used the Building Blocks to think through what to do with his business (he sold the major assets to another company) and then to decide on a future career.

Ken focused his analysis of what kind of work to look for by asking himself, "Why is a decision necessary? Because I've sold my business and want to keep working. What needs to be determined? The best kind of work for me." Here is the list of Criteria Ken developed:

Achieve
    Helping people who want help
    Personal involvement
    A managing or counseling position
    Demonstrable results
    A feeling of accomplishment
    Intellectual challenge and stimulation

Preserve
    Financial security
    Close relationship with family and friends
    Leisure time for golf, swimming, religious activities

Avoid
    High pressure
    Frequent travel
    Office politics

His choices included starting another business, managing someone else's business, and working as an employment counselor. He ruled out the first two options because they didn't meet his Criteria of helping people, preserving his leisure time, and avoiding high pressure.

At this writing, Ken is senior counselor with a nationally known executive search agency. And though he recently turned 70, he has no thoughts of retiring. "This is the most rewarding work I have ever done," he says. "My experience in business gives me a perspective that the other counselors lack, and I have instant credibility with our clients. I hope to keep going as long as I have a contribution to make."

You may think Ken was lucky. If so, his luck was the product of three factors: his good health, his determination to find meaningful work at age 57, and his decision to use the Building Blocks to clarify his objectives and focus his search for meaningful work.

In this book we have seen how the Seven Building Blocks can help people make big decisions (a change of careers) and small ones (a gift for a wedding); resolve problems (a commotion in a store, a dispute over taking out the garbage); and create opportunities (the sale of a house to a buyer who didn't have enough cash for a downpayment). We have seen how a new company president overcame resistance to his appointment and got his management team to work with him rather then against him, and how a young woman decided between marriage and a law degree.

If you are concerned about bringing about a change in your own life, use the Building Blocks to clarify your Purpose and to discover innovative ways to achieve it. Ask a friend to serve as your sounding board. If your decision affects other people, try to involve them in thinking through your decision. *Shared Solutions are better than solo Solutions.*

The systems for managing change that is demonstrated in this book work for executives in business and government essentially because they work for people. Make the Building Blocks work for you, starting today. You can control your own future. If you've learned the Building Blocks and have the determination to use them, *make up your mind!*

# Appendix A

# GLOSSARY

**Absolute requirements**    The Criteria that you judge so important that any Solution absolutely has to satisfy them to be acceptable.

**Achieve, preserve, and avoid**    The elements used in establishing your Criteria. By asking "What do I want to achieve, preserve, and avoid as problems by any decision I make?" you identify your Criteria.

**Alternatives**    Possible decisions or choices from which you select the one (or more) that best fulfills your Purpose.

**Criteria**    Standards or objectives by which you develop and evaluate possible Solutions.

**Decision**    The Alternative or Solution that best fulfills your Purpose by meeting each of your absolute requirements and doing an outstanding job on your desirable objectives.

**Desirable objectives**    Criteria that are less important than your absolute requirements and that may not be satisfied by your eventual decision. As with absolute requirements, they help you generate and evaluate the Alternatives.

**ExecuTrak Systems**™    Systems for managing change, of which the Seven Building Blocks for decision making are a fundamental part. These systems have been applied extensively by men and women in industry and government (see Appendix C).

**Issue**    A gap between what *is* happening and what *should be* happening, or between what *is* or *should be* happening and what *could be* happening (good or bad). Asking "Why is a decision necessary?" and applying these three Criteria—*is*, *should be*, and *could be*—helps to smoke out the Issues.

**Matrix**    A chart used to evaluate Alternatives. On it are recorded the Purpose, Criteria, Priorities, Alternatives, and data used to assess the Alternatives and select the one or more that best satisfy your Purpose.

**Objectives**    See **Criteria.**

**Priorities**    Criteria that have been separated into absolute requirements and desirable objectives, with a value indicating the relative importance of each desirable objective.

**Purpose**    What you are trying to determine. Your statement of Purpose describes your mission—what you want your decision to achieve.

**Rating**    The numerical weight assigned to an Alternative in assessing how well it meets each Criterion.

**Solutions**    See **Alternatives.**

**Total**    The sum obtained by adding up the scores for each Alternative. An Alternative that scores at least 15 percent better than any other tentatively becomes the "Winner," provided it is not weak on any of the highly rated desirable objectives. Before making a final choice among Alternatives, consider how to overcome the apparent winner's shortcomings or combine the characteristics of several Alternatives to create a better and more innovative Solution.

**Troubleshooting**    Examination of your decision to anticipate what could go wrong and to prevent, minimize, or overcome the adverse effects.

**Value**    The numerical weights assigned to a desirable objective in assessing its relative importance.

**Value rating**    The score obtained by multiplying the value of each Criterion by the rating of each Alternative. This score reflects your judgment of how well each Alternative satisfies each Criterion.

# Appendix B

# Checklists of Criteria
# for Personal Decisions

**BUYING A NEW CAR**

A.  **Costs**
    1.  Trade-in allowance on old car
    2.  Price; terms of financing
    3.  Operating expenses
        a. gasoline—type used (regular, premium, no lead) and EPA mileage ratings
        b. routine servicing requirements*
        c. frequency of repair cost*
    4.  Insurance
    5.  Resale value*
B.  **Accommodations and Comfort**
    6.  Passenger capacity
    7.  Interior space (leg room, head room, seat padding, ease of entry/exit)
    8.  Smoothness of ride
    9   Noise level
    10.  Luggage capacity
    11.  Maximum rated load
C.  **Handling Ability**
    12.  Maneuverability (ease of steering, cornering ability, turning radius)
    13.  Peppiness (responsiveness, acceleration, passing ability)

*Ratings by *Consumer Reports* and other services are available in most libraries.

D.  **Dependability**
  14.  Frequency-of-repair record*
  15.  Availability of parts, knowledgeable mechanics
  16.  Convenience of service
  17.  Reputation of service facility
  18.  Warranty coverage
E.  **Safety**
  19.  Crashworthiness*
  20.  Braking ability*
  21.  Visibility by other vehicles
  22.  Potential hazards (protruding objects in dashboard, blind-spots)
  23.  Rating of tires
F.  **Psychic Income**
  24.  Image/prestige (sporty, utilitarian, luxury)
  25.  Feeling from ownership
G.  **Additional Features**
  26.  Options
  27.  Availability by a certain date
H.  **Other Factors**
  28.  Auto sales excise tax
  29.
  30.
  31.
  32.


## BUYING A HOUSE

A.  **Location**
  1.  Accessibility (proximity to work, shopping, schools, friends, family, recreation, public transportation)
  2.  School quality and attendance trend (likelihood of school being closed or consolidated because of declining enrollment)
  3.  Neighborhood
       a. stability (house turnover rate, zoning changes, planned highway or other public facilities)
       b. noise
       c. traffic congestion
  4.  Liens on property or public rights of way
B.  **Taxes and Upkeep**
  5.  Property tax level and outlook

      6.   Insurance rates for homeowner's policy (and car insurance if rate depends on location)

      7.   Utilities and maintenance

C.  **Condition**

      8.   Structural soundness

      9.   Condition of roof, gutters, storm windows, basement (wet or dry), drainage, foundation, insulation, heating and air-conditioning system, hot water, freedom from termites or rodents

    10.   Major improvements needed

D.  **Space and Comfort**

    11.   Play area—internal (playroom, finished basement) and external (yard)

    12.   Space for entertaining (dining and living room area sufficient for guests)

    13.   Layout and traffic pattern (proximity of kitchen to dining area, convenience of bathrooms, accessibility of kitchen to street for carrying groceries)

    14.   Closet and storage space

    15.   Adequacy of bedrooms, bathrooms, showers

    16.   Adequacy of car-storage space (garage, driveway)

    17.   Cabinet space (kitchen and/or dining room)

    18.   Adequacy of electricity (location of outlets, load capacity)

    19.   Potential for future expansion (addition, conversion of attic to bedroom)

E.  **Other Factors**

    20.   Friendliness of neighbors

    21.   View

    22.   Status

    23.

    24.

## CHOOSING A COLLEGE

A.  **Academic Standards**

     1.   Accreditation

     2.   Admission requirements

     3.   Degrees offered

     4.   Selectivity of admissions

     5.   Professional qualifications of faculty (percentage of Ph.D.s, schools attended)

     6.   Placement of graduates

B. **Costs**
   7. Tuition
   8. Room, board, books, fees
   9. Transportation .
   10. Financial aid (grants and loans)
   11. Part-time employment opportunities

C. **Curriculum**
   12. Academic requirements
   13. Courses of study offered
   14. Variety of offerings in area(s) of interest
   15. Opportunities for specialized training or research
   16. Opportunity for independent study or travel

D. **Student Body**
   17. Size of student body
   18. Faculty-student ratio
   19. Coeducational or sex-segregated

E. **Campus Atmosphere**
   20. Variety of campus activities
   21. Emphasis on intramural and competitive sports
   22. Competitiveness
   23. Social life
   24. Religious affiliation and activities
   25. Proximity to other colleges and universities
   26. Restrictions on personal freedom

F. **Personal Services**
   27. Personal guidance and counseling
   28. Medical care
   29. Academic advisory system
   30. Job placement and counseling

G. **Other Factors**
   31.
   32.


# DRAWING UP A FAMILY BUDGET

A. **Fixed Expenses**
   1. Taxes
   2. Life insurance
   3. Health insurance
   4. Car insurance
   5. Social security
   6. Pension deductions
   7. Union or professional dues

8. Mortgage payments or rent
9. School tuition
10. Car payments
11. Loan repayment (personal, home improvement)
12. Other fixed expenses (nursing-home care, alimony)

B. **Variable Expenses**
13. Food (including lunches and dining out)
14. Clothing (including laundry and dry cleaning)
15. Medical expense
16. Transportation
   a. automobile—gas, oil, maintenance, repair, garage rent, parking fees, tolls
   b. mass transit—bus and train fares
   c. taxi
17. Home operation (heat, cooking, electricity, water and sewer, rubbish service, telephone, cleaning materials, household help, yard and garden)
18. Maintenance (furniture and appliance repair or replacement)

C. **Self-Improvement**
19. Instruction (music, dance, scouting)
20. Magazine and book subscriptions
21. Personal grooming
22. Entertainment
23. Recreation and hobbies
24. Children's allowance

D. **Charitable Contributions, Gifts, Family Presents**

E. **Reserve Fund (Savings)**
25. Calamities (major illness, death, unemployment, major home repair)
26. Children's education
27. Discretionary items (vacation, home improvement, retirement investment)

F. **Other Factors**
28.
29.

# Appendix C

# Professional Applications

The Executrak methodology described in this book has been used by men and women in business, industry, and government to resolve such issues as:

BUSINESS PLANNING
1.  Acquisition: Determine best way to transform an adversary takeover into a successful marriage.
2.  Merger: Determine best way to integrate worldwide operations.
3.  Divestment: Determine best way to accomplish Supreme Court-ordered divestiture of major business while optimizing competitive position and return on investment.
4.  Depressed earnings: Determine best way to insure rapid turnaround of earnings picture.
5.  Consolidation: Determine best allocation of facilities to shrink costs.
6.  Strategic planning: Determine best way to develop an effective five-year strategy and plan for all company operations; determine best way to strengthen strategic planning and interaction between parent company and European subsidiaries.

MARKETING
1.  Products: Determine the most appropriate strategy for North American marketing of products; determine best way to insure successful implementation of strategy.
2.  Market share: Determine best way to insure increased market penetration.
3.  Contract bid: Determine best way to acquire $90 million contract in the face of keen competition.
4.  Advertising: Determine most effective advertising strategy to follow.

## MANUFACTURING

1. New operations: Determine best way to get new plants on stream by targeted date.
2. New products: Determine best way to insure new product quality and reliability in the marketplace.
3. Yields: Determine best way to increase manufacturing yields and spur productivity growth.

## ORGANIZATIONAL STRUCTURE AND DEVELOPMENT

1. Product development: Determine most appropriate research organization to implement new product and product development strategies worldwide.
2. Interaction: Determine and insure successful reporting relationships between corporate staff and profit-center groups.
3. Coordination: Determine best way to coordinate worldwide research.
4. Commitment: Determine best way to win commitment of all senior management to charters and objectives, and to insure accountability and measurable result.
5. Synergy: Determine best organizational realignment to take advantage of potential synergy across product lines.

## FINANCIAL PLANNING

1. Cash flow: Determine best way to insure increased cash flow.
2. Cost reduction: Determine best way to significantly reduce costs without adverse impact on key operations.
3. Taxes: Determine best (legal) way to return profits from foreign operations while minimizing tax burden.
4. Receivables: Determine best way to significantly reduce receivables without contaminating customer relationships or sales.
5. Paperwork reduction: Determine best way to significantly reduce paperwork and financial reports.
6. Capital investment: Determine best way to win reprieve from freeze on capital investment.

## LABOR RELATIONS

1. Negotiating leverage: Determine best way to strengthen negotiating position with union, customers, and vendors.
2. Strike operations: Determine best way to minimize dislocations and continue operations during strike.

3.   Manpower development: Determine best way to insure development and effective implementation of manpower needs inventory and a manpower organization planning and development program.

4.   Effective interaction: Determine best way to insure effective interaction between corporate personnel and plant workers.

### GOVERNMENT RELATIONS

1.   Legislation: Determine best way to respond to new government legislation while minimizing adverse impact on company.

2.   Combatting criticism: Determine best way to respond to government attacks on industry and company.

3.   Reconciling differences: Determine best way to insure that government agencies reach agreement on divisive issues.

### COUNSEL TO SENIOR EXECUTIVES

1.   Issue resolution: Identify and determine how best to resolve major issues facing executives newly promoted or "parachuted in" from outside the company.

2.   Revitalization: Determine best way to revitalize the organization; develop a "common vision" among members of the management team.

### MISCELLANEOUS

1.   Budget cut: Determine best way to respond to government edict cutting departmental budget by 20 percent.

2.   Oil crisis: Determine best way to get major oil cartel to reduce prices.

3.   United Nations: Determine best way to manage United Nations task force.

# Index

logical functions of brain, 11
lying, as choice in decision making,
    6

Maier, Norman, 26n.
management, role of, in decision
    making, 14–16
Mann, Leon, 26n.
marriage, disintegration of, 137–151
middle managers, 180
midlife, changing careers in,
    180–190
mission, see purpose
motherhood, choice of, decision-
    making skills and, 152–158
motivation, increased by
    positive thinking, 18

necessity
    of decisions, questioning of,
        40–43
    of troubleshooting solutions,
        98–99
needs
    budgetary, 122
    in ranking desirable objectives, 69
    for status, perquisites and, 14–16
numerical qualification
    of absolute requirements, 71
    see also ranking; ranking of
        criteria

occupations, statistics on change of,
    180
opportunity, statement of purpose
    as, 57
opportunity criteria, 111
options, exploration of, 83

perquisites, status needs and, 14–16
personal crises, decision-making
    skills and, 137–151, 158
persuasion, power of, 9
perversity, law of, 100
positive thinking
    failure to troubleshoot solutions
        and, 98
    pitfalls of, 17–23

powerlessness, feelings of, 14
power of persuasion, 9
preservation, as criterion
    in choosing motherhood, 154–155
    in decision making, 193
    establishment of, 59–63
    in instant analysis, 107–108, 112
    in job planning, 161, 164
    in reentering workforce, 171
    in setting priorities, 66
    in solving budgetary problems,
        132
    in solving marital problems, 143
prevention of potential problems, 97
preventive action, 21
principles of decision making, 8
priorities
    assignment of, in budgeting, 123
    establishment of, as decision-
        making skill, 26, 31–32, 65–73,
        192
    establishment of, in reentering
        workforce, 168
    poorly established, 76
    reordering of, in career changes,
        185
    use of, in personal decision
        making, 11
problems
    definition of, 40–52
    perception of, 53–54
    troubleshooting of, 97
protective action, 21
protective criteria, 111
purchasing decisions, decision-
    making skills and, 123, 127, 133
purpose, criteria and, 59–64
purpose, establishment of
    in budgeting, 123, 130, 132
    in job planning, 162, 166–167
    in personal decision making,
        119–120
    in reentering workforce, 171–173
purpose, statement of
    in career changes, 184
    in choosing motherhood, 154
    in decision making, 26, 28–31,
        53–58, 78, 191